Lewis
paul
Tsurumaki
marc
Lewis
david j.

Situation Normal...

Pamphlet Architecture 21

Princeton Architectural Press
New York

Published by
Princeton Architectural Press
37 East Seventh Street
New York, NY 10003

2 1 00 99 4 3 2 1 First edition

For a free catalog of books by Princeton Architectural Press, call 1.800.722.6657 or visit www.papress.com.

Book and cover design: Paul Lewis, Marc Tsurumaki, and David J. Lewis
Editor: Mark Lamster
Special thanks to: Gina Bell, Jane Garvie, Caroline Green, Clare Jacobson, Therese Kelly, Annie Nitschke, and Sara E. Stemen of Princeton Architectural Press—Kevin C. Lippert, publisher

Printed in the United States

Library of Congress Cataloging-in-Publication Data
Lewis, Paul, 1966-
Situation Normal-- / Paul Lewis, Marc Tsurumaki, David J. Lewis.
p. cm. -- (Pamphlet architecture ; 21)
ISBN 1-56898-154-6 (pbk. : alk. paper)
1. Lewis-Tsurumaki-Lewis. 2. Architectural design--Research.
I. Tsurumaki, Marc, 1965– . II. Lewis, David J., 1966– .
III. Title. IV. Series: Pamphlet Architecture ; no. 21.
NA737.L454L48 1998
721--DC21 98-39325
CIP

testing 1..2..3.. installation: StoreFront for Art and Architecture, 1997

ens . plazas . offices . curtain walls . wheels . I-beams . flag poles . high hats . window washers . ashtrays . smoking lounges . putting greens . bru

ry carts . convenience stores . machine rooms . offices . apartments . front doors . elevators . trucks . shelving . supermarkets . receptions desks

s . drawers . pivots . handles . hinges . doors . slide projectors . peepholes . jambs . lenses . faucets . knobs . knockers . letter slots . pulls . do

out counters . mannequins . tri-vision signs . display racks . revolving doors . spiral stairs . ladders . handrails . display windows . cash

y desks . front doors . parking spaces . loading docks . sidewalks . payphones . floor plates . lobbies . mailboxes . benches . potted

ols . counterweights . running tracks . bench presses . stairmasters . treadmills . free weights . diving boards . showers

stics . wheels . seats . seats . foam . lights . triggers . wires . speakers . pullies . chairs . walls . microphones . tracks . motor

screens . escalators . popcorn . ticket booths . vcr tapes . video stores . cineplexes . trash containers . toilets . ramps . previe

apartments . offices . strip windows . hippodromes . suspended ceilings . elevators . fluorescent lights . marinas . promenades . observ

. ceilings . pipes . joists . stools . springs . light tables . peepholes . bushings . cables . lights compression springs . oval sleeves . scales

CONTENTS

photo: Jim Hughes for the *Daily News*

snafu

Coined during the early years of World War II, the acronym *snafu*—a condensation of the phrase "situation normal all fucked up"—was used by American soldiers to describe a condition of disorder created by an excess of conflicting Army rules and regulations. Absorbed into vernacular speech, its profanity largely forgotten, the term *snafu* now signifies a general state of confusion, disruption, and system breakdown. Computer glitches, traffic jams, and bureaucratic red-tape are common examples of what are today considered *snafus*. In a culture fixated on efficiency, speed, and information exchange, *snafus* are anathema to progress and production.

Lost in contemporary usage of the term, however, is the tension held in the original phrase between two seemingly incompatible conditions occurring simultaneously: the normal and the fouled-up. If something is normal, everyday, and ordered then how can it also be disordered, jumbled, and otherwise out of kilter?

The fouled-up condition arises not from the insertion of a foreign agent into the system, but as a result of the very structures of the system itself. In its original meaning, *snafu* refers to that moment when a deviation, latent in the system, occurs, subverting the intended outcome of the given system. In the Army, a *snafu* was created when the rigid rules and carefully choreographed routines of military life produced chaos and disorder—the very conditions that they were designed to avoid.

This original meaning of *snafu* as an ironic paradox has been lost. The existence of foul language, requiring the use of an acronym in civilized speech, has resulted in the erasure of the original phrase. Also lost is the challenge to the very legitimacy of rules and order posed by the inherent paradox of the wording. This challenge arises from the possibility that beneath the surface of the normal or the familiar exists the strange or the unfamiliar; the possibility that what is considered normal must, by definition, include the abnormal.

The ten projects presented in this pamphlet are predicated on the original understanding of *snafu*, and exploit the potency of the unfamiliar that lurks behind the facade of familiarity. We propose tactics of architectural inquiry into the normal and the quotidian. By exacerbating the logic of the conventional, the presumably rational elicits the unexpectedly irrational latent in the everyday. This approach enables a speculative, implicitly critical way of thinking through the tacit assumptions of contemporary architecture.

TACTICS

The meaning of the term *snafu* resonates with Michel de Certeau's concept of tactics, which he opposed to the idea of strategies.[1] Strategies demand locations of power, require competition, define

A **snafu** *disrupts flow and creates a traffic jam.*

legitimate modes of research, and establish the boundaries of acceptable practice. Strategies are the institutional processes that set norms and conventions. Architecture has always been defined by strategies—witness Vitruvius's writings on the orders of architecture; Diderot's reclassification of the orders in his *Encyclopédie*; Le Corbusier's five points; and the recent codes of New Urbanism.

Tactics, on the other hand, lack a specific location, survive through improvisation, and use the advantages of the weak against the strong. In particular, tactics are the modes of creative opportunity that operate within the gaps and slips of conventional thought and the patterns of everyday life. Tactics turn the logic of the strategy against itself within the space established by that strategy. In the discourse of architecture, for instance, tactics are not constructed out of an opposition to a prior architectural strategy or a call for a new architectural style or form. Instead, tactics indicate a method of thinking through conventions of architecture, not *de facto* solutions or conclusions to given situations. Our work employs tactics that seek to provoke the logically irrational by inducing plays and slippages between form, function, and program.

FUNCTION

Is it possible to rekindle the architectural potential of *program*, a term whose denigration coincided with the proclaimed failure of modern architecture to sustain the demands of "form follows function"? Program can easily become a reified, unexamined square-footage designation that is shoved into form—an act euphemistically called "programming the building." The challenge faced in reclaiming function is to escape the limits imposed on it by the paucity of contemporary rationality as defined by scientific positivism and economic necessity.

What if the terms of investigation—*form* and *function*—were reversed? What if the relation between the terms was fraught with self-conscious ambiguity, forcing a perpetual inquiry into the habits, habitats, and associations of each? In other words, what happens if "form follows function" is replaced by "function fucks with form?" Here, function is not reducible to form, and form is not the inevitable conclusion of programmatic dictates. Instead, a self-critical, imaginative, recombinative conception of function opens up a new territory for formal and spatial exploration.

Formal issues are reopened to an association with issues of function, but one not seeking a linear or singular conclusion, answer, or progeny. While seemingly privileged in this new pairing, function is actually placed in a self-conscious position: an agent whose identity and actions can be called into question. The success of this new productive coupling lies in the establishment of a relation that is inherently critical of the conventions and familiar positions assumed by both terms as part of the design process.

photo: Fondation Le Corbusier

photo: William Turner

photo: Georgia van der Rohe

photo: C.A. Thompson—The Capital Times

Masters *prescribe lessons of architectural strategy. From top to bottom: Le Corbusier, Louis I. Kahn, Mies van der Rohe, Frank Lloyd Wright.*

The **Habbakuk***: an aircraft carrier made from ice and wood pulp.*

Buried in the annals of military inventions, the Habbakuk exemplifies this productive coupling. Designed in 1943 by Englishman Geoffrey Pyke, the Habbakuk was an ocean vessel made from ice mixed with wood pulp, producing a compound called Pykrete. Pykrete was the perfect solution to the wartime shortage of steel. It was plentiful, durable, and melted slowly. Winston Churchill gave his support to such military icebergs when a test chunk of Pykrete refused to melt in his bathtub. The Habbakuk was to be 2,000 feet long with 50-foot-thick walls and a giant refrigeration plant. Unfortunately, frigid labor conditions prohibited the completion of this perversely functional mating of water and ice.[2]

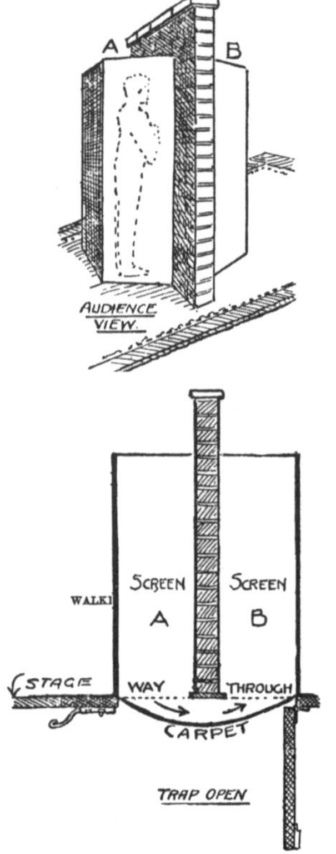

Prior to a performance, **Houdini** *called attention to the function of the brick and mortar wall by having it constructed by the best masons in town. This emphasis provided the camoflauge for the illusion of walking through the wall. In fact, Houdini slipped under it.*

J. C. Cannell, The Secrets of Houdini *(New York: Dover, 1973), 43.*

CONVENTION

This new coupling of function and form enables a creative foray into conventions and the conventional. Conventions of architecture are the aspects of the discipline that are taken for granted through daily repetition and habit. This includes both the formal and the functional aspects of architecture: from conventional form and conventional thinking about form to assumed functional constraints and uses. If strategies of architecture seek to establish, fix, and propagate conventions and norms, then tactics seek to examine how conventions become conventional, who they serve, and what they maintain. This tactical maneuvering within the conventions of contemporary discourse requires a recognition of the complex values, political imperatives, social codes, and economic constraints that coalesce in the process of normalization. Generic programs—stores, bars, apartments, office buildings, theaters—provide a rich ground for examination, for these "dumb programs" possess recognizable architectural conditions.

Because of its embeddedness in economic and social systems, architecture is inevitably tied to convention. Beyond the conduct of architects, a great many factors constrain architecture, insuring that it remains within disciplined boundaries, from formal codes of behavior to preset functional assumptions.[3] In the last century, an entire publishing industry has developed around the conventions of architecture, serving the needs of the architectural profession with titles such as *Architectural Graphic Standards* and *Time Saver Standards.* While such conventions are meant to aid the practice of architecture, architectural conventions often insure that tenuous social constructions, such as the unstable boundary between public and private, remain unexamined.

The case of the single-family bomb shelter exemplifies the power of architectural conventions. During the two decades following the detonation over Hiroshima, the idea of the single-family home as vulnerable without a nuclear bomb shelter was mobilized in government policy to help facilitate the normalization of the atomic bomb.[4] Under the auspices of various civil defense programs, the single-family bomb shelter was used by the American government to persuade its populace that a nuclear exchange was survivable. Grafted into the policies of postwar suburbanization, it translated the new and unfathomable nuclear technology into a digestible aspect of everyday life. Like the den or the TV-room, the single-family bomb shelter was depicted as just another room that should be added to the modern suburban house. By playing within the conventional codes of home and house, the single-family bomb shelter helped domesticate nuclear technology, contributing to an acceptance of an ideology of the Cold War that required that the looming possibility of nuclear exchange become part of normal, daily existence.

Our interest in the commonplace and the normal is distinct from other attempts to inscribe value to architecture through the presumed authenticity embodied in the ordinary or the found object. In these other strategies, citations of the everyday, whether signage or common form, are brought face-value into a project in the hope of reconnecting architecture to a larger audience through elements of the vernacular. Although these everyday-architecture strategies privilege the familiar as knowledge worthy of study, the unavoidable pitfall of these literal uses of the everyday arises from the paradox of basing a design strategy on work whose value resides precisely in the fact that it was not designed by architects. Repetition of the familiar, with the assumption that the familiar is equivalent to a greater collective consciousness, does not form a critical practice. As Friedrich Nietzsche stated: "What is familiar is what we are used to; and what we are used to is most difficult to 'know'—that is, to see as a problem; that is, to see as strange, as distant, as 'outside us.'"[5] A critical architecture challenges the familiar, seeking out what has been forgotten in the making of the conventions and norms of generic, everyday architecture.

Suburban Nuclear Bomb Shelters
Architectural conventions used to domesticate nuclear war.

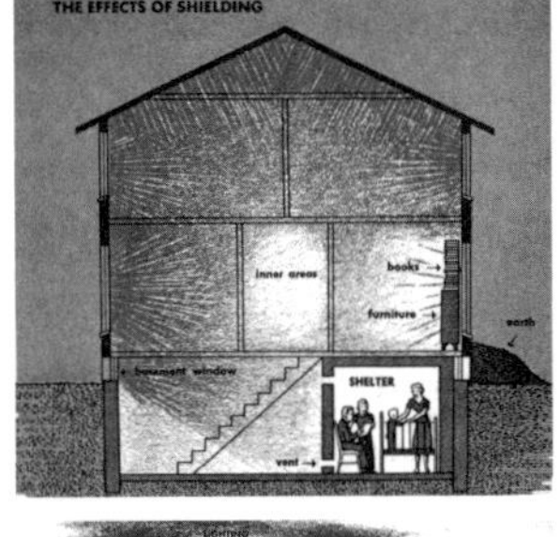

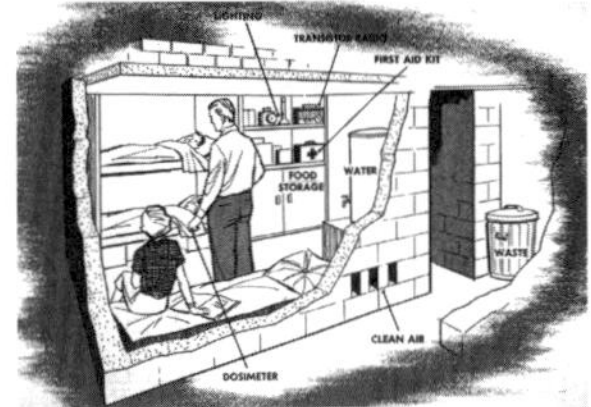

House section and detail from Survival in a Nuclear Attack: Plan for Protection from Radioactive Fallout, *report to Governor Nelson A. Rockefeller, New York State, 1967.*

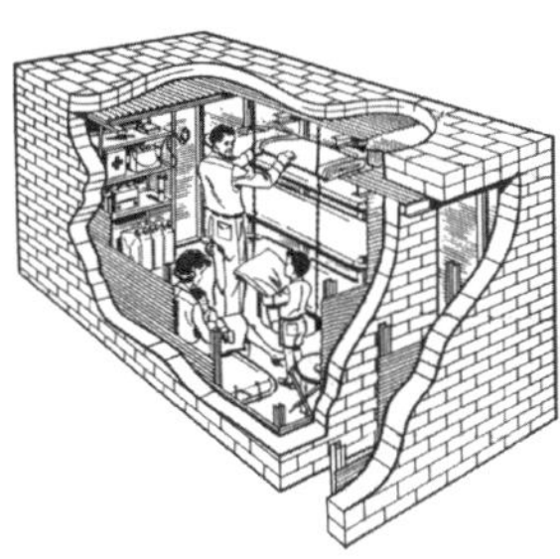

Do-it-yourself shelter from the Surviv-All *catalog, 1962.*

Shelter used as gardening surface from Life, *15 September 1961, 106.*

photo: Ralph Morse for *Life*

photo: Underwood + Underwood/Corbis

Fay Wray *poses for a publicity shot at a Hollywood mini-golf course.*

LOGIC

> *"How did logic come into existence in man's head? Certainly out of illogic, whose realm originally must have been immense."*
> – Friedrich Nietzsche, *The Gay Science* [6]

The subjects of our examinations range from the domestic object to urban space: from a simple chair to a Manhattan block. While the subject changes, the tactics of investigation remain consistent. Each project begins with a close inspection of an existing situation, triggering a speculative "What if..." question that postulates an alternative derived from the logic of the given object of study. For example: "Given the inevitable existence of eavesdropping in art galleries, what if eavesdropping itself was the catalyst for an art installation?" Each question frames an inquiry that resonates with the conventions of the situation. The point is not then to design the unusual, since the very idea of the unusual is an already identifiable concept with set parameters. Rather, the point is to exacerbate the logic of the given situation to illuminate that which is already strange within it. In this understanding of logic we mean the chain of justifications and assumed connections that conspire to insure the continued reign of habits.

This design tactic requires a double-edged approach to the logic of the conventional. First, the question used to begin the speculation ("What if...") raises to the fore the logic that sustains the norm. For instance, assumed in the question "What if a video store and an urban multiplex were cross-bred?" is an inquiry into the norms that separate these mutually dependent entertainment outlets. Second, the speculation (combine video and film) sets into motion a sequence that is used to produce the project. The logic for this sequence is then derived from the given logic of the architectural conventions in question (video store and multiplex). Slips, chance matings, induced exchanges, delirious inventions, and causal juxtapositions are all used as possible provocations to rationally produce a speculative trajectory for design. Each project logically pursues the latent perversity of architecture to near illogical ends: rational thought pushed to the limits of rationality.

Fay Wray's miniature-golf slippers illustrate this process. Popular during the Great Depression, mini-golf was the result of a combination of fiscal restraint and excessive free-time: an inexpensive and domesticated version of tees, fairways, and greens. The linear action of putting, a radical reduction in scale, and a need to entertain resulted in the barrage of fantastic figures, forms, and obstacles that constitute the image of mini-golf. So popular was mini-golf in the early 1930s that Hollywood stars staged photo shoots on courses, producing a set of unforeseen juxtapositions. Fay Wray's high-heeled shoes—essential accouterments of the star—were incompatible with the manicured terrain. Mini-golf slippers to be placed over high heels were thus introduced to resolve the potential conflict. The redundant footware was illogical in isolation but perfectly acceptable in this mating of Hollywood and miniature-golf.

Instead of designing the golf-course, what if one concentrated on producing the architectural equivalent of the slippers?

Mini-golf ***slippers*** *for the high-heeled: negotiating between the fashion of publicity shoots and delicate putting surfaces.*

SURRATIONALISM

> *"We still live under the reign of logic...but the methods of logic are applied nowadays only to the resolution of problems of secondary interest. The absolute rationalism which remains the fashion permits consideration only of those facts strictly relevant to our experience."*
>
> –André Breton, "Manifesto of Surrealism"[7]

A portable vacuum producing apparatus, patented by Alexander Mackenzie Jack in 1912. The mating of bellows and shoes allowed the house to be cleaned by walking.

One project of surrealism was the bringing of Freud's theories of the unconscious to bear on society and culture through the arts. Specifically, dreams and automatism were deployed by surrealists in an attempt to undermine bourgeois notions of stability and coherence predicated on the undisputed agency of the conscious individual. Today, surrealism is largely consumed by the very social structures it sought to undermine. Domesticated by easily digestible pop-culture interpretations and mass-market reproductions, surrealism has been reduced to simplistic associations with dreams and the supernatural.

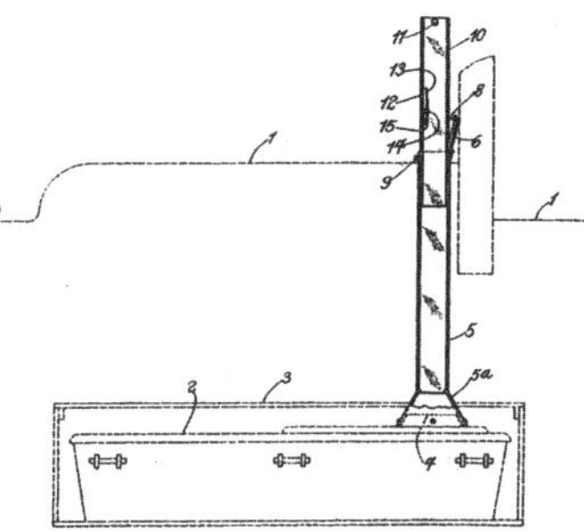

An attachment for caskets, patented by Jacob Fishman in 1922. An inverted periscope provides for visual connection to the deceased after burial, complete with casket light and locking cover.

While surrealism operates in the ambiguous territory at the limits of the real, surrationalism is the self-conscious examination of the rational. Writing on the concept of surrationalism, Gaston Bachelard maintains that "all Surrational forms must be produced by intellectual reforms."[8] Surrationalism is first and foremost a conscious, critical, and rational project, its goal being the liberation of rationality from the encrusted habits of convention. As opposed to indulging in dreams, automatism, and unqualified chance, surrationalism seeks a creative logic to engender disquieting associations between or within the everyday. If surrealism seeks to explore the more-real-than-real world behind the real, then surrationalism uses rationalism to test the boundaries of rationalism itself. If the dream-inspired images, objects, and paintings of surrealism were necessary to manifest a reality beyond itself, then surrationalism demands a tactical method of operation, a process, a way of thinking through givens. The image as end-product is displaced in favor of a surrational mode of inquiry.

A gun barrel for shooting around corners.

photo: David Scherman for Life

In this sense, architecture is an inherently surrationalist activity, but one that has forgotten the basic indulgences of the act. Architecture begins with a projection onto the world of an image that is foreign to it. This image is then made material through a highly ritualized act, legitimated at each stage through claims to rationality. Before it is built, a building is conceptualized through drawings, a process that dictates the organization of the project according to a hyperrational sequence: from schematic design to design development; from construction documents to construction administration. Reduced to routine, the ontological surrationalism of architecture is removed from contemplation, quarantined into the bowels of normal habit. Perhaps the processes of acceptable architectural practice are not what they appear, but are a professional defense against the inescapable fissures that can be revealed through a surrationalist inspection of architectural reason.

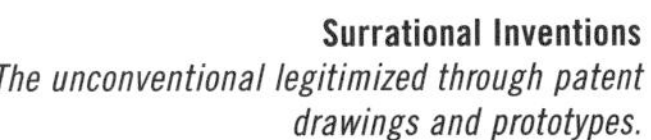

Surrational Inventions
The unconventional legitimized through patent drawings and prototypes.

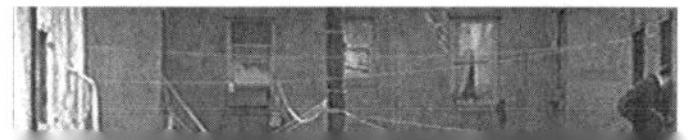

GREAT STONE FACE

The silent films of Buster Keaton offer a precedent for this surrational tactic, the taking of a logical sequence to the brink of illogic. Keaton develops a chain of events built on a slip, a twist, or a deviation from the expected. His cinematic wit arises out of the contradiction between his logical actions and the illogical, almost absurd conclusions they bring about. Keaton's bewildered reaction, his trademark stone-faced, emotionless response to situations, announces his obliviousness to the *snafu*, while revealing to the audience the discrepancy between expected and actual conclusions. Precisely because Keaton adheres to proper rules and codes of conduct, the conclusion is never what it should be.

Caught on the third floor of a tenement building in *Neighbors*, Keaton wants to be with his love in a room directly across a back alley. By having two neighbors, located on the floors below him, step out of their respective windows at the same time, Keaton forms a human ladder. The vertical section of the tenement building is used to create the solution to the gap that separates Keaton from his love. This unorthodox yet logical solution to an ordinary problem sets up an entire series of delirious connections and situations that drive the remaining narrative of the film.

This tranformation of given, ordinary conditions is a consistent motif of Keaton's films. In the short film *The Scarecrow*, Keaton plays with the paradox of the fence as barrier and door. Here, a door is created as characters open a gap in the hinged picket slats. Still, the proper code of using a door is maintained as the gap is shut by the last person leaving, returning the fence to its original configuration.

Keaton's comedy is more than frivolous entertainment. As Freud has written, the joke allows one to break with social decorum, publicly revealing taboos through an acceptable medium of transgression.[9] The transgression enacted in Keaton's work lies in the nuanced play between the expected and the illogical. Plots are generated by entirely reasonable deviations from the ordinary. Conclusions, however, are completely in keeping with the sequences of events established during the film, often a tumultuous convergence of mini-narratives. In contrast to visually aggressive films that rely on the production of obvious difference and bombastic puns, Keaton's subtle manipulations offer a tactic that we seek to draw into architectural thought.

TESTING 1...2...3...

In comparison to film, there exists the possibility in architecture for switching between modes of representation: between drawing, model, text, installation, and built project. If surrational projects exacerbate the logic of architectural conventions, then the representation of these projects must also play upon the conventions of architectural representation. *Mantel Piece*, an installation completed for the Architectural League of New York–Young Architects Forum Exhibition of 1997,

Facades generate a human ladder.
***Buster Keaton*, Neighbors, *1922*.**

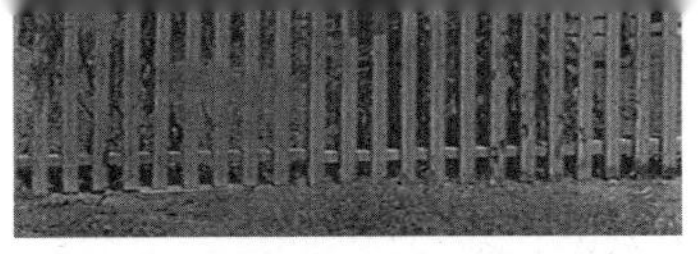

served as an early testing ground for representational cross-fertilization. *Mantel Piece* began with a speculative curiosity that arose from the restrictions of the given wall space for display: a blocked-up fireplace with a residual mantel piece and mirror. In order to produce a presentation surface, the mantel was extruded horizontally 3 feet into the gallery. Four motorized models were attached to the presentation surface, with the mirror providing a view to the rear of the models. Drawings placed horizontally under the models were anamorphically stretched to correct for the inevitable distortion caused by viewing the drawings laid flat at the height of a mantel (5 feet 3 inches). The glow from a red neon bulb inserted under the table substituted for the absent fire.

During the summer of 1997, the ten projects that comprise this publication were exhibited at the StoreFront for Art and Architecture in New York City, under the title *Testing 1..2..3...* For the show, each project occupied a standard 4-foot by 8-foot board (see pages 2-3). Attached to each board was a 2-inch speaker, a digital answering machine, and a start button on the end of a steel bar cantilevered out from the board into the space of the gallery. Pushing the button activated an answering machine that played back a verbal description of the selected project, thus engaging the viewer both aurally and visually.

For the exhibition, the standard method of presenting static models cloaked under Plexiglas was replaced by the display of models connected to slowly revolving motors, illustrating the operation of the projects through the seduction of auto-erotic mechanical repetition. Models and drawings were sutured together, producing an overlap between these two representational techniques. Projects that were once presented as full-scale installations were represented through model and drawing, reversing the assumed progression from drawing to model to built work. Two projects, *Slip Space* and *Pull-of-Beauty*, environments for other shows previously installed at StoreFront, were presented so that they reversed the hierarchy between object and frame. In both, the original location of the installation was marked and then connected to a model of StoreFront into which a model of the installation was inserted. A representational oscillation was sought between original, model, and the installation location.

SITUATION NORMAL...

As the installation of these projects explored the conventions of the gallery, the printing of the projects within the limitations of this book elaborate upon the ways in which architectural representations confer legitimacy. To do this, the projects illustrated here engage the strange oscillation between being works in themselves and projections of future construction, an oscillation inherent in much architectural representation. The measured accuracy and precision of architectural models and drawings, executed through sections and plans, and orchestrated by the dissection of the whole into isolated details, makes future constructions believable. Unlike other artistic mediums,

A fence doubles as a door.
***Buster Keaton*, The Scarecrow, *1920*.**

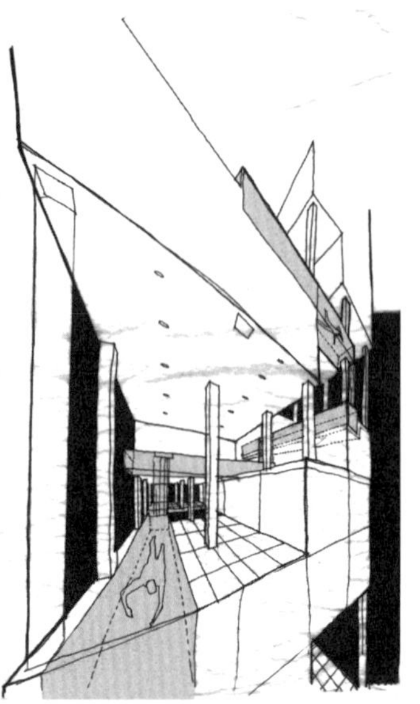

Project #13: **Mies Core Towers**
Midtown, New York. Stacking and pinwheeling Mies's speculative courtyard houses produces a vertical dwelling with a spiral void. Water from one pool spills down to the next, creating a fifty-story domestic waterfall.

Project #19: **Taxi Stand**
Houston Street, New York. The physical necessities of car and driver are combined with a taxi museum at the northern edge of SoHo: showers for drivers are located over a car wash; taxi drop-off; auto-repair; gas; lounge; and club.

the conventions of architectural representation bestow an unprecedented legitimacy on what is represented, however irrational or perverse. Our deployment of architecture's legitimizing codes parallels surrealist painting's use of a highly-realistic technique to construct the uncanny believability of their surreal visions.

In addition to using conventional drawing techniques—plan, section, elevation, perspective, axonometry—in isolation to legitimate these surrational projects, drawing formats are combined to creatively examine the assumptions and limitations of conventions usually kept in isolation. Orthographically-projected-plan-sectioned-isometrics (*Exquisite Corps Clothing Store*), isometrically-exploded-sections (*Container Building*), and multiple-sectioned-perspective-plans (*Free Lobby.Block 1290*), for instance, produce multiple and simultaneous readings not available in typical drawing formats. These hybrid drawing forms are produced by combining hand-executed techniques with digital technology, thus exploring the possibilities ignored in the race for the immaculate digital image. In these representations, human figures—traditionally used either as detached referents for scale or as decorative applique—are placed in the work to explicate the intended operations of the projects. These figures are carefully choreographed to illustrate specific bodily engagements. As an integral part of the representation, the figures enable a reading of these projects that simultaneously combines the formal and the functional norms called into play.

Each project has been redrawn and reworked to exploit the possibilities derived out of the restrictions of the print medium. Rather than surrendering to the limitations of the book format, the conceptual trajectory of each project is crossbred with the linear nature of the book. The representations for a project are sutured together by conceptual lines that begin at the project title. Photographs of models are overdrawn and drawing formats are combined to take advantage of the two-dimensional printed page. As a publication, this pamphlet aspires to be more than just a collection of projects. *Situation Normal...* exemplies the pleasures of surrationally engaging the logic of conventions embodied in architecture and its representation.

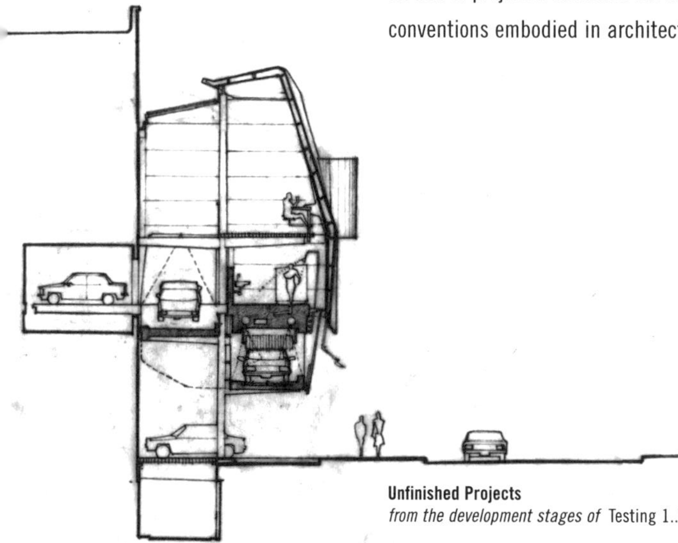

Unfinished Projects
from the development stages of Testing 1..2..3..

NOTES

1 Michel de Certeau, *The Practice of Everyday Life* (Berkeley: University of California Press, 1984).

2 Francis Russell, *The Secret War* (New York: Time Life Books, 1981), 178–9.

3 For a further discussion of the concept of discipline in the historical development of the discourse of architecture see Mark Wigley, "Prosthetic Theory: The Disciplining of Architecture ," *Assemblage*, (1991), 6–29.

4 David J. Lewis, "Domesticating Nuclear War: The Discipline of Architecture and the Single Family Nuclear Shelter," (Masters thesis, Cornell University, 1992).

5 Friedrich Nietzsche, *The Gay Science*, trans. Walter Kaufmann (New York: Vintage Books, 1974), 301.

6 Ibid., 171.

7 André Breton, "Manifesto of Surrealism," in *Manifestoes of Surrealism*, trans. Richard Seaver and Helen R. Lane (Ann Arbor: University of Michigan Press, 1972), 9.

8 Gaston Bachelard, "Surrationalism," as quoted in Julien Levy, *Surrealism* (New York: De Capo Press, 1995), 188.

9 Sigmund Freud, *Jokes and Their Relation to the Unconscious*, trans. James Strachey (New York: W. W. Norton & Company, 1960). For a discussion of the social politics of humor and architectural change, see Arnold Lewis, "Domesticating Change through Humor," in *An Early Encounter with Tomorrow: Europeans, Chicago's Loop, and the World's Columbian Exposition* (Urbana: University of Illinois Press, 1997), 46–8.

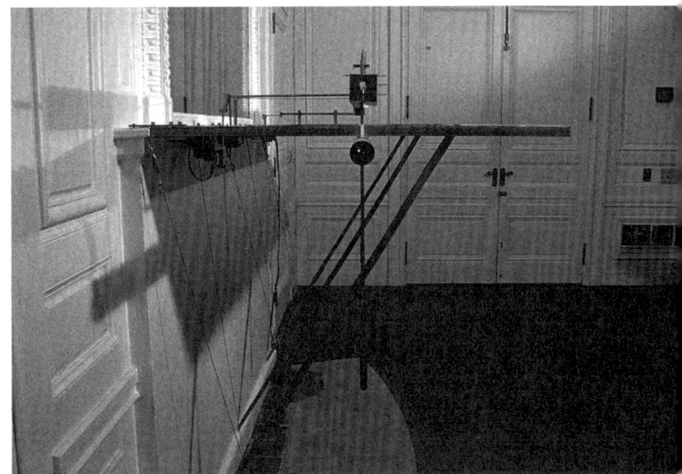

Mantel Piece, *Architectural League of New York–Young Architects Forum Exhibition, 1997*

What if the different notions and configurations of *containers* in office and residential units, grocery stores, and transportation systems were reconfigured to maximize efficiency? Here, the elevator core, typically buried within a building, is brought to the exterior facades, to serve as front door, reception lobby, picture window, and bridge to the street-level store. Semitrailers delivering goods to the grocery store are hydraulically lifted from the basement level and opened up, becoming the store's shelves and thereby mitigating the cost and time of unloading and restocking. Above, each floor-through unit is split by a mobile utility core, dividing the space into an apartment and an office. By moving this core, rapid changes in the economy can be matched by instantaneous redistribution of the space allocated to each renter's live and work areas.

container building

***site:* Lower East Side through-block**

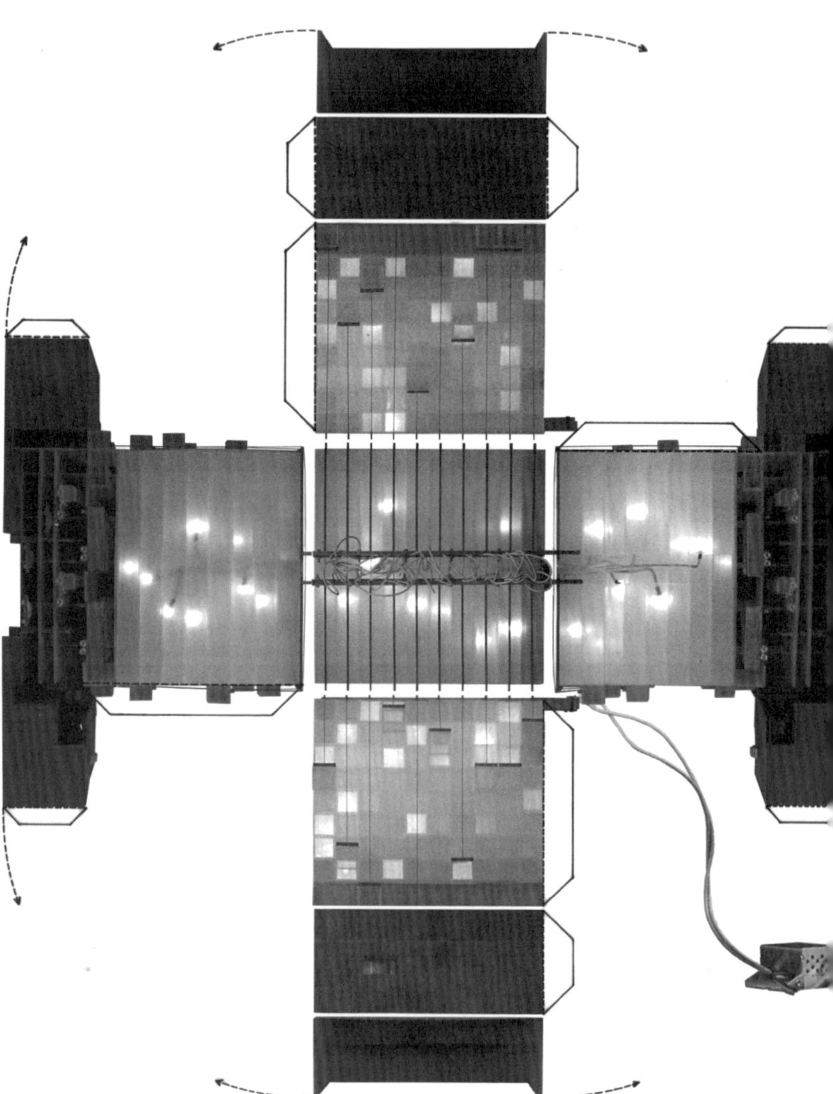

container model package

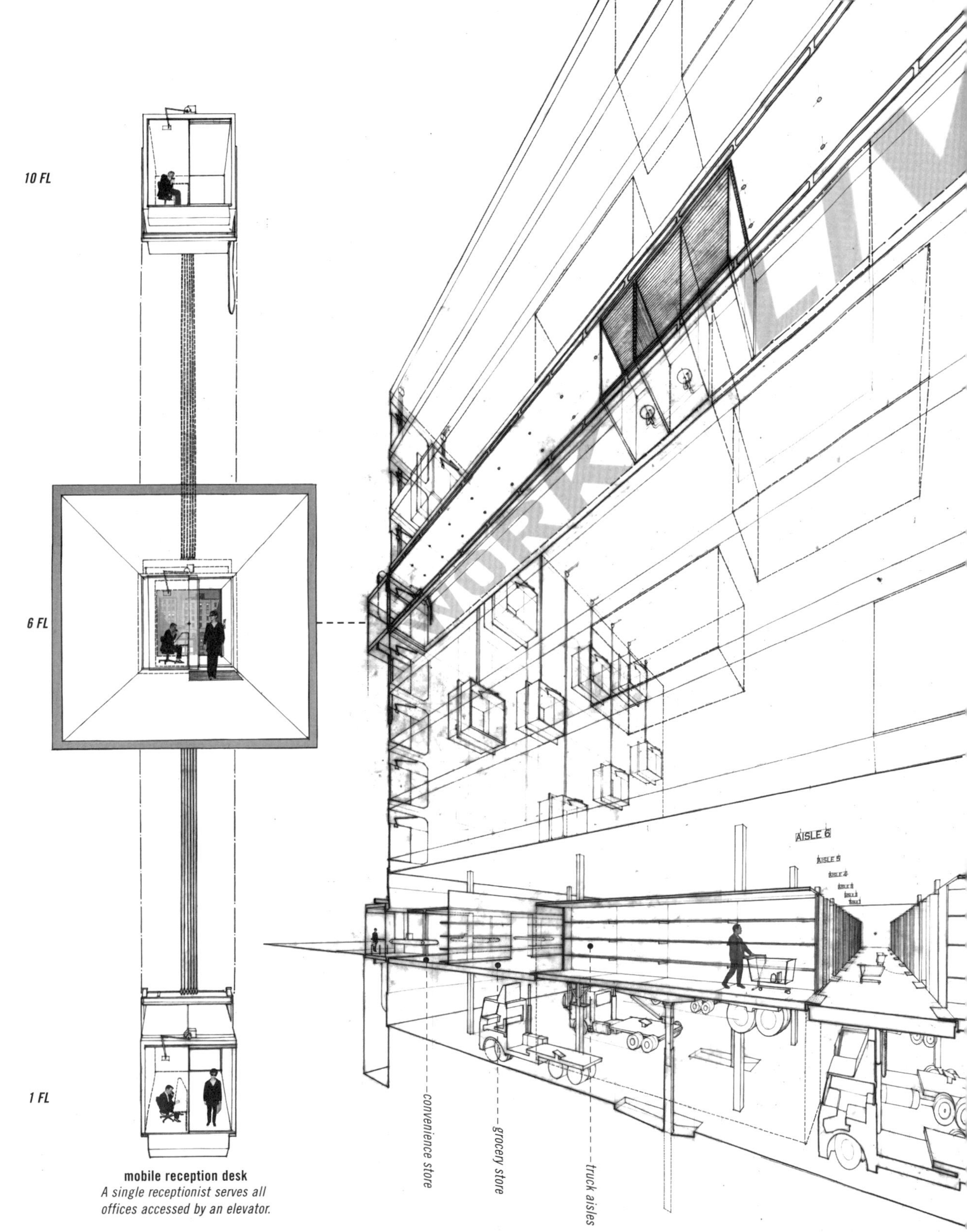

mobile reception desk
A single receptionist serves all offices accessed by an elevator.

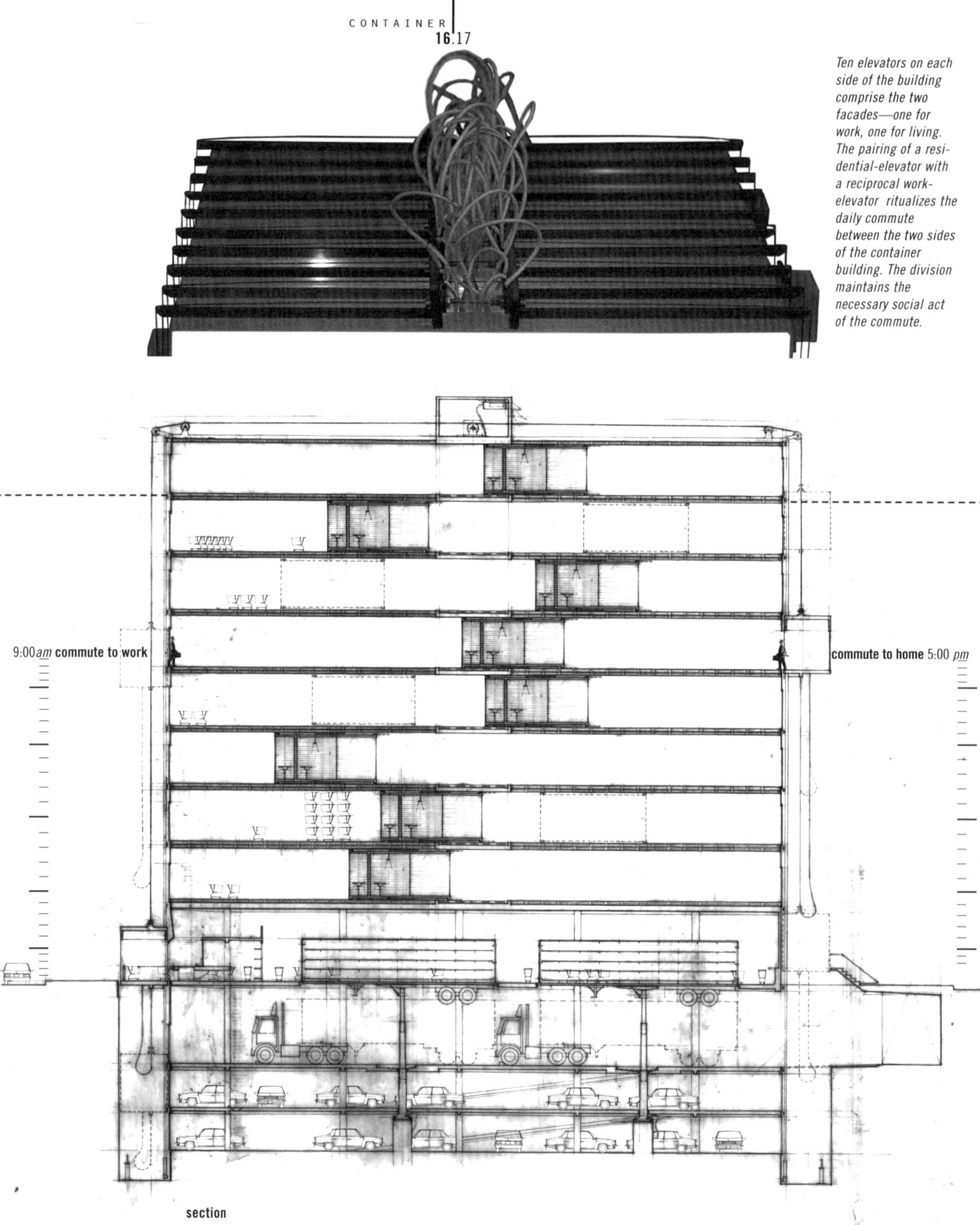

Ten elevators on each side of the building comprise the two facades—one for work, one for living. The pairing of a residential-elevator with a reciprocal work-elevator ritualizes the daily commute between the two sides of the container building. The division maintains the necessary social act of the commute.

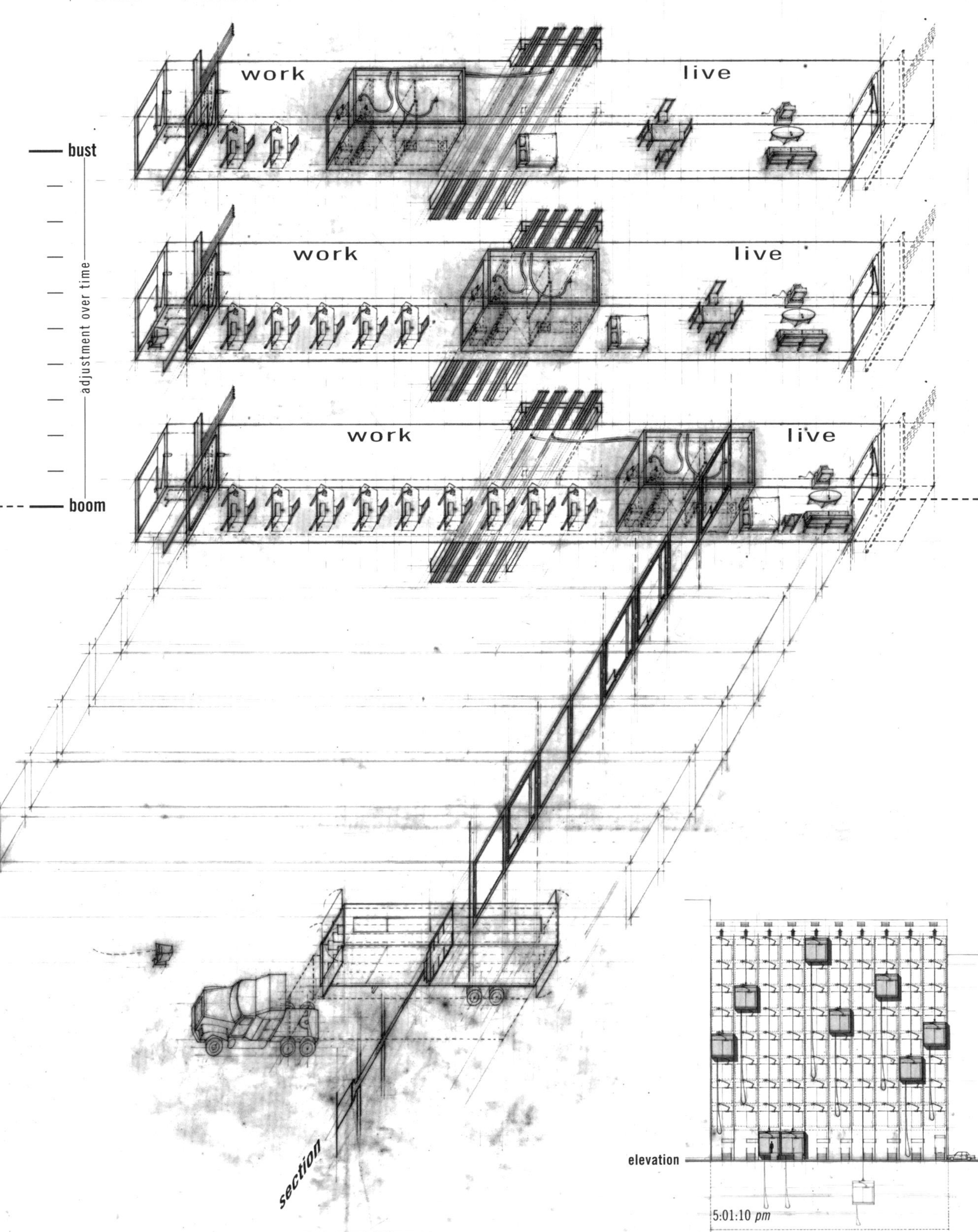
work
live
work
live
work
live
bust
adjustment over time
boom
section
elevation
5:01:10 pm

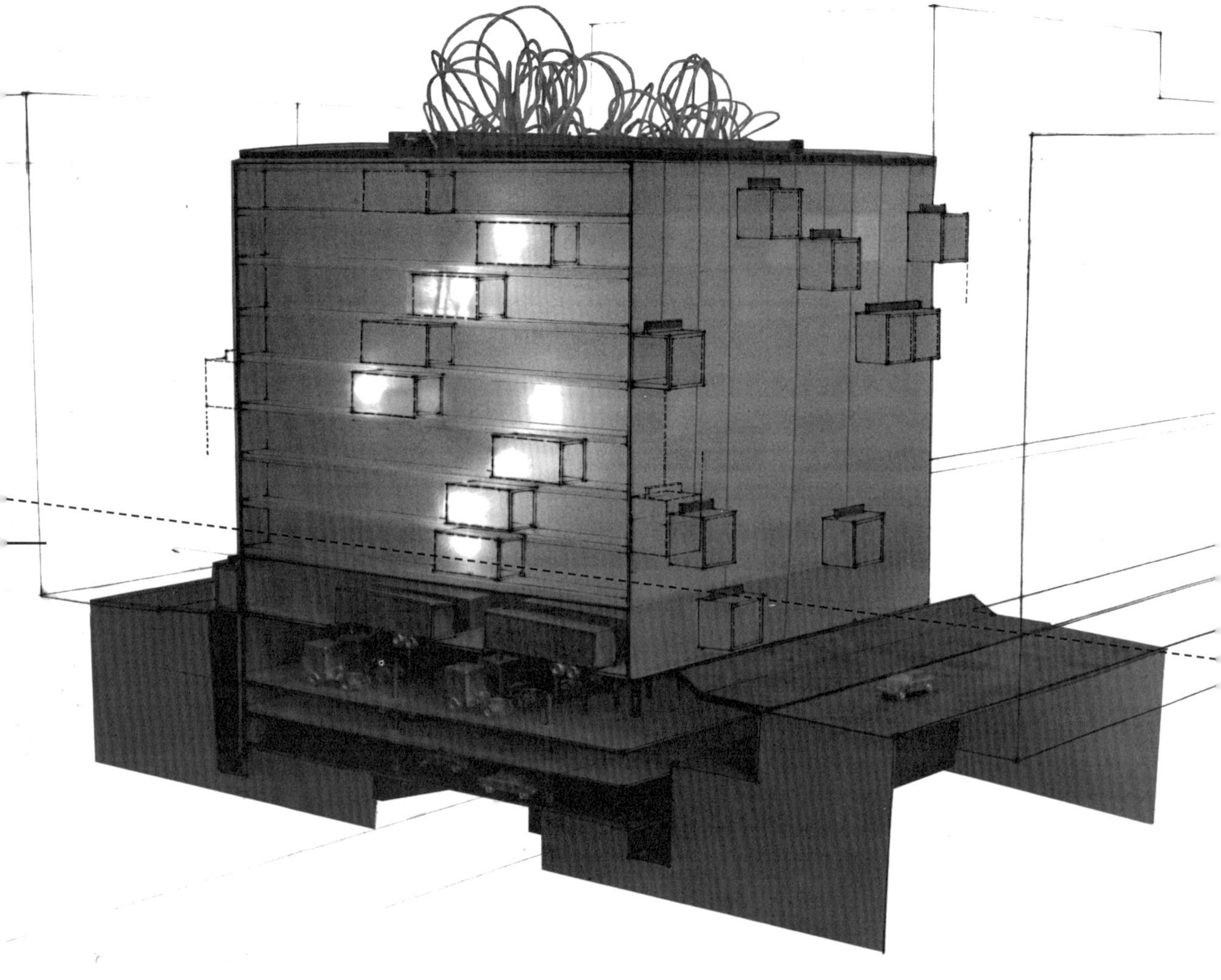

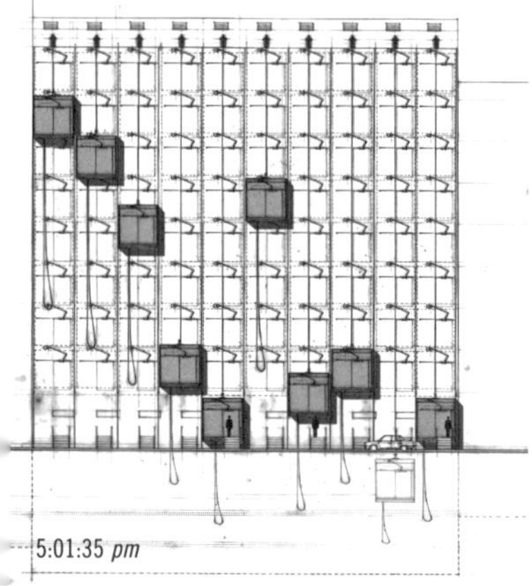

5:01:35 *pm*

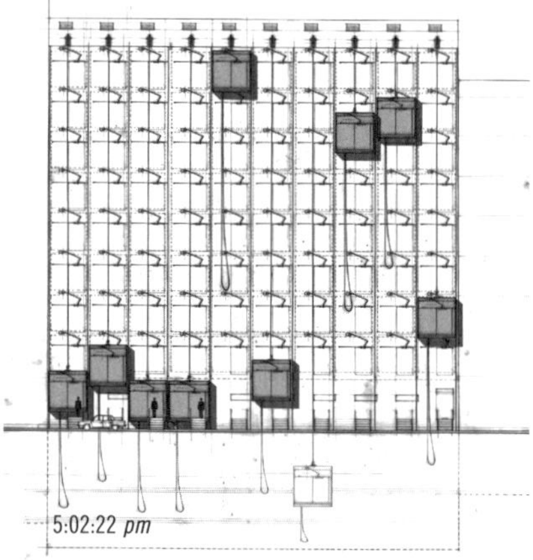

5:02:22 *pm*

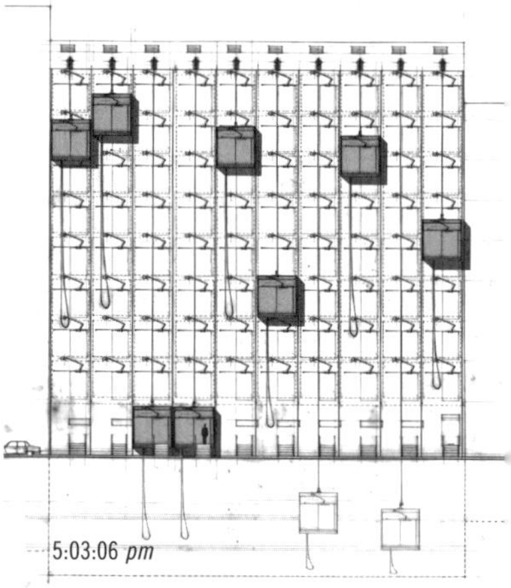

5:03:06 *pm*

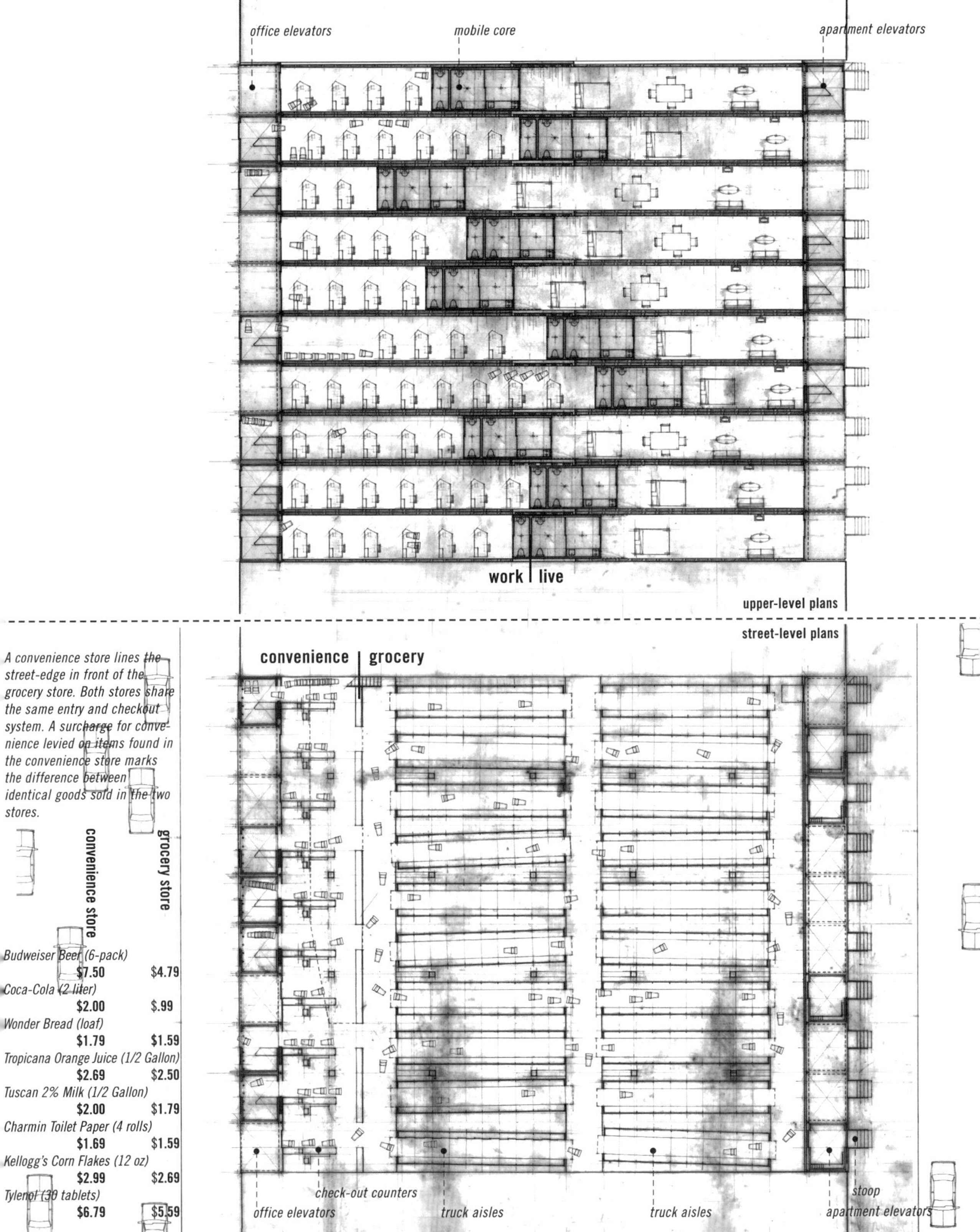

A convenience store lines the street-edge in front of the grocery store. Both stores share the same entry and checkout system. A surcharge for convenience levied on items found in the convenience store marks the difference between identical goods sold in the two stores.

	convenience store	**grocery store**
Budweiser Beer (6-pack)	**$7.50**	**$4.79**
Coca-Cola (2 liter)	**$2.00**	**$.99**
Wonder Bread (loaf)	**$1.79**	**$1.59**
Tropicana Orange Juice (1/2 Gallon)	**$2.69**	**$2.50**
Tuscan 2% Milk (1/2 Gallon)	**$2.00**	**$1.79**
Charmin Toilet Paper (4 rolls)	**$1.69**	**$1.59**
Kellogg's Corn Flakes (12 oz)	**$2.99**	**$2.69**
Tylenol (30 tablets)	**$6.79**	**$5.59**

"...it in the other side and put your ear..."

"...since Warhol, its tiring and a perpetual..."

"...yeah, I mean, like, he was just like..."

"It'll just be 45 minutes, are you coming to...."

"Listen, if you can't stand still mommy's gonna..."

"Did you hear what she said about this stuff?"

"Isn't that the gallery director who..."

"Is this one famous....mmmm its beautiful..."

"...what I heard was wrong, in my opinion..

in my opinion..

oustics . wheels . seats . foam . lights . triggers . wires . speakers . pullies . chairs . walls . microphones . tracks . motors . amplifiers . cables . spotlights . plas

eavesdropping

***site:* Exit Art/The First World**

The most seductive conversation is the conversation overheard. Eavesdropping, a one-way transgression of the boundary between private and public, is a time-honored tradition of the art gallery event. This project takes this transgressive social act and ritually enacts it within the public space of a gallery. As a mechanism that constructs the process of eavesdropping, the installation plays with the desire to *listen-in* to a private conversation, bringing it into public consciousness. By exacerbating the spatial conditions of eavesdropping, the installation catches the individual at the moment of complicit interaction. Ten chairs on wheels with 12-foot-high backs form a continuous wall in their closed position. On the gallery wall directly in front of the seats are ten isolated, low volume speakers. The speakers are connected to a remote microphone suspended in the middle of the gallery. The microphone dangles overhead from a motorized pulley that slowly moves it across the gallery, scanning conversations. These private words are amplified and relayed to the ten speakers. Convoluted acoustical foam on the inside of the chairs create a sound isolation room between the chairs and the speaker wall, allowing the sitter to eavesdrop on the gallery.

plan

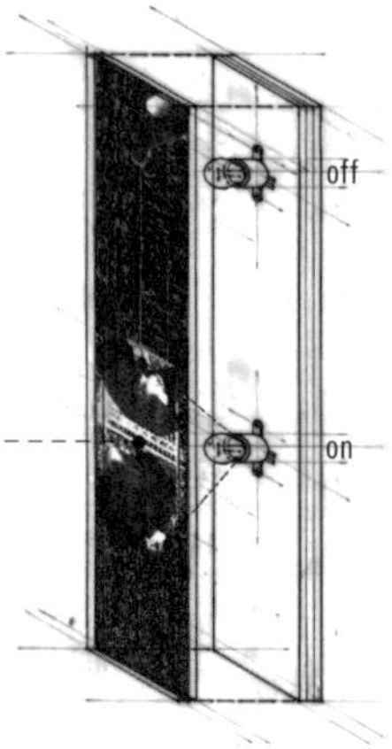

A touch-pad switch on the chair seat triggers a light on the gallery-side of the chairs, notifying those in the gallery of an eavesdropper. The light also illuminates an image imbedded in the chair that illustrates the act of eavesdropping. The combination of sound and vision across the wall of chairs demonstrates the complicitous interaction of everyone in the gallery.

photos: Michael Moran

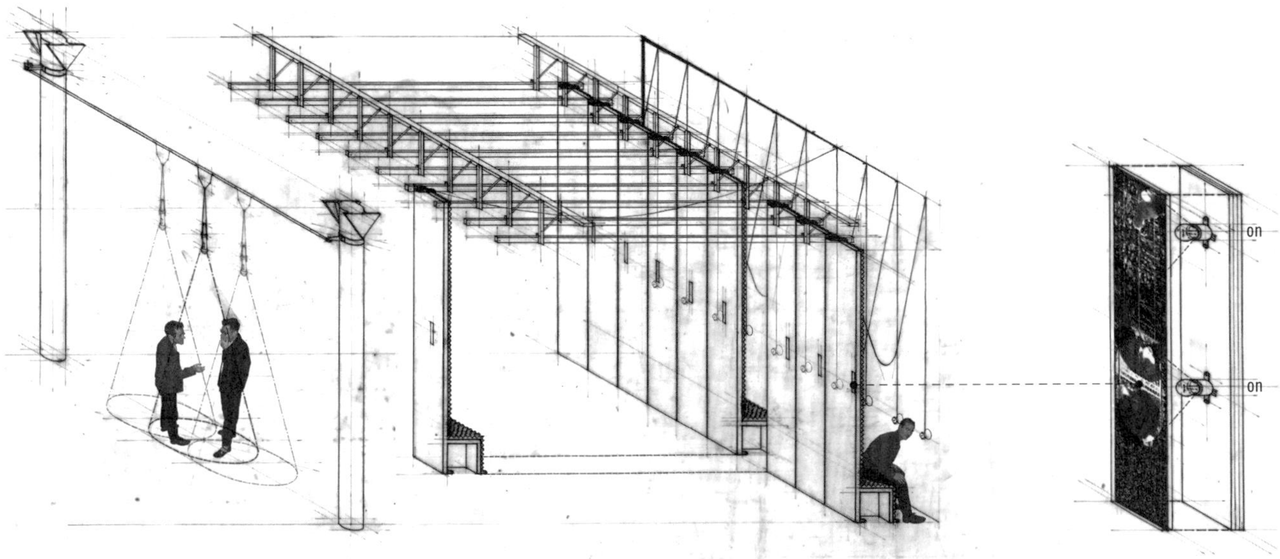

A ceiling track enables each chair to move back and forth. When a chair moves, the solid wall that provides the acoustical isolation necessary for eavesdropping is disrupted. As the pieces are randomly moved, the eavesdropping mechanism becomes dismantled, replaced by the formal pleasure of chairs of absurd proportions.

1 *chair image*

2 *chair image*

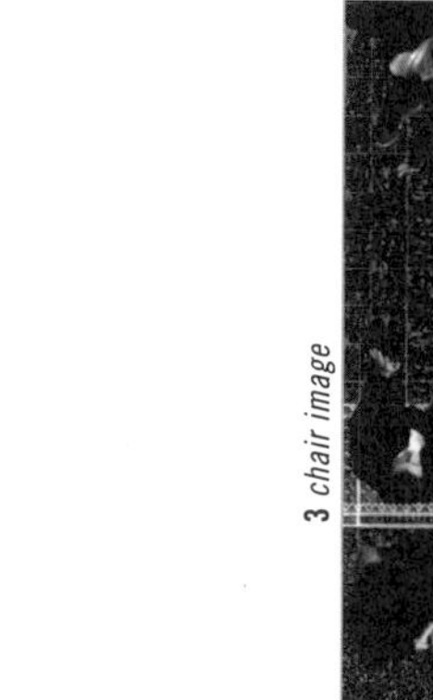

3 *chair image*

4 *chair image*

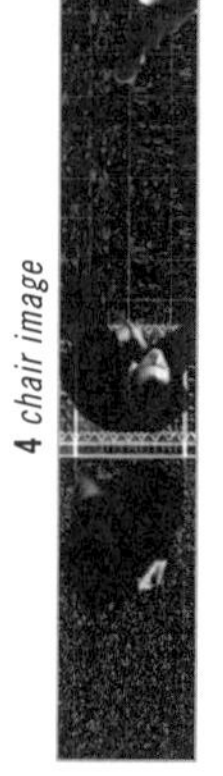

5 *chair image*

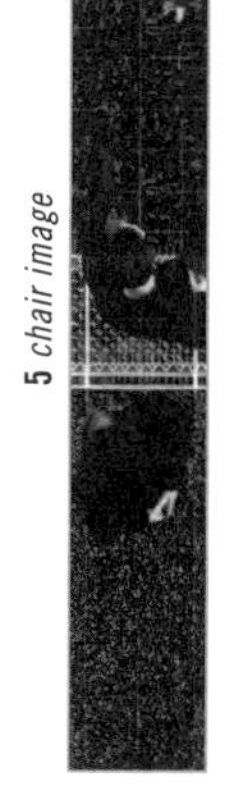

photos: Michael Moran

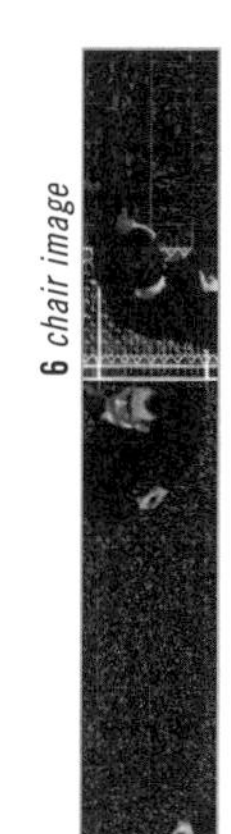
6 chair image

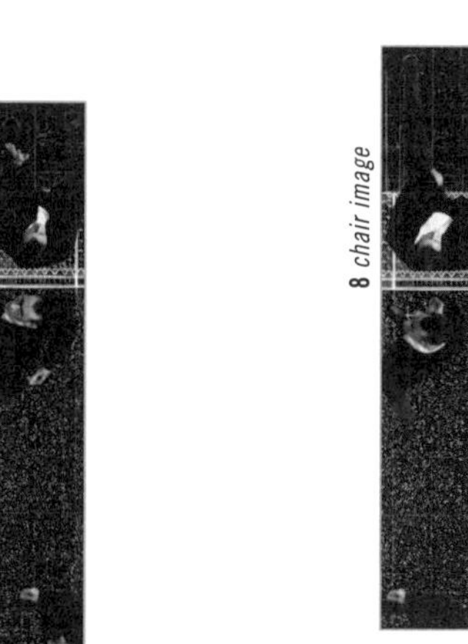
7 chair image

8 chair image

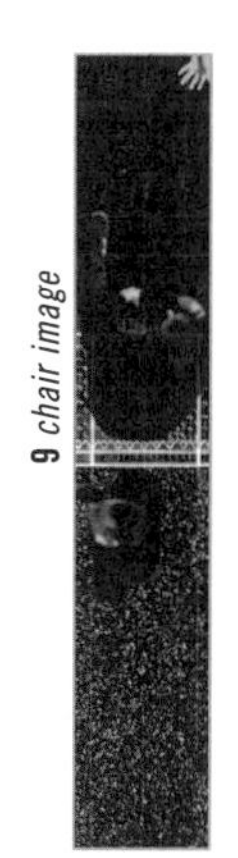
9 chair image

10 chair image

exquisite corpse clothing store

***site:* East 53rd Street**

A clothing store is a redolent breeding ground for daily enactments of the game of *exquisite corpse*. Following the logic of the division of the body, the store is split into four linked shops: shoes, pants, shirts/jackets, hats. Each is entered through an oversized, 30-foot wide, perpetually revolving door that blurs window shopping, browsing, and entry into a seductive mix. A spiral staircase in the center of the door spins continuously, allowing one to circulate vertically without changing location in plan: an updated Archimedean screw. The changing rooms at the mezzanine level are cantilevered over the street, allowing customers to test public reactions to selected clothing. Tri-vision signs on the outside of these changing rooms rotate, creating an oscillation between a wall of clothing-specific advertising and a screen of vertical slots allowing momentary glimpses into the interior of the rooms.

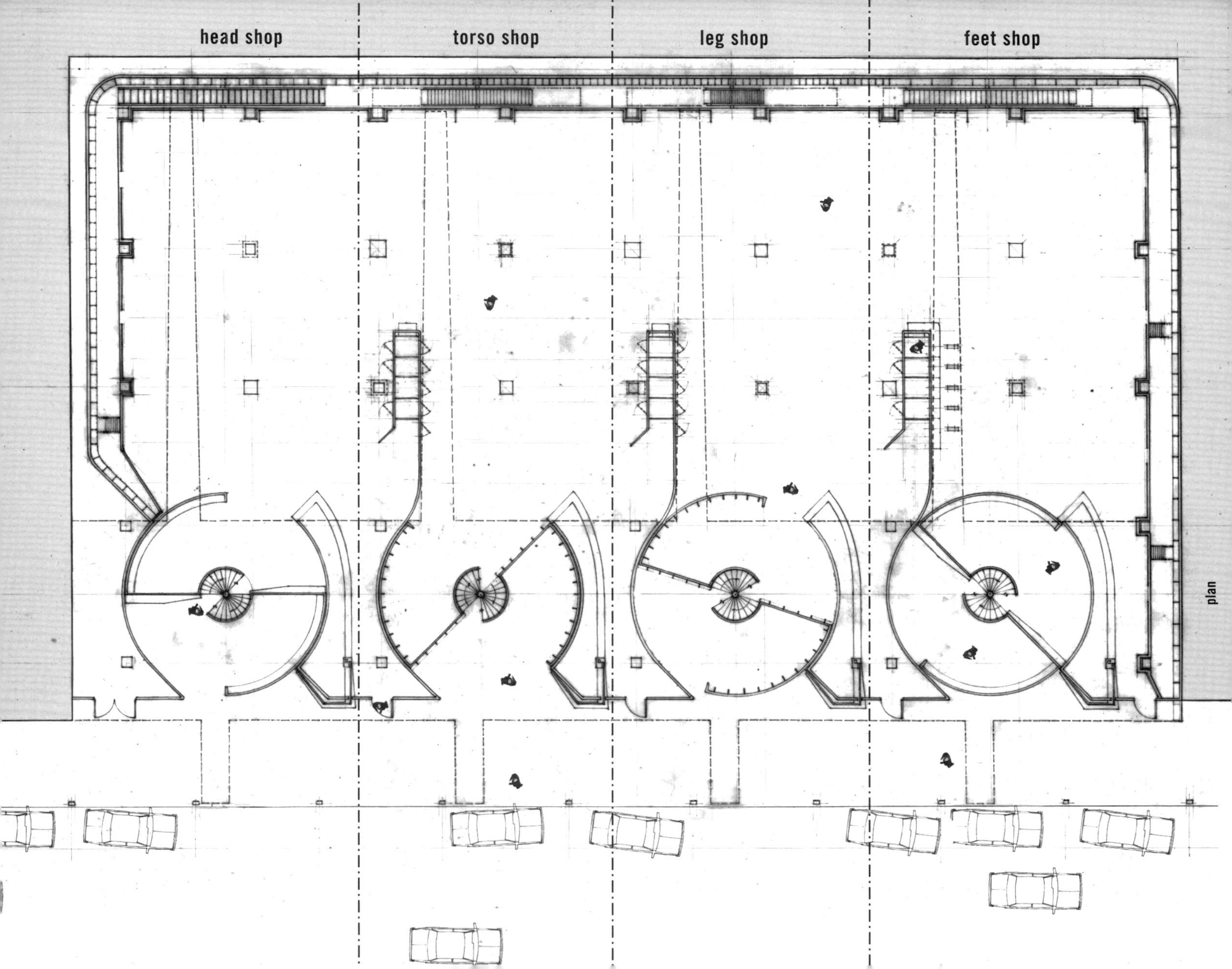

plan

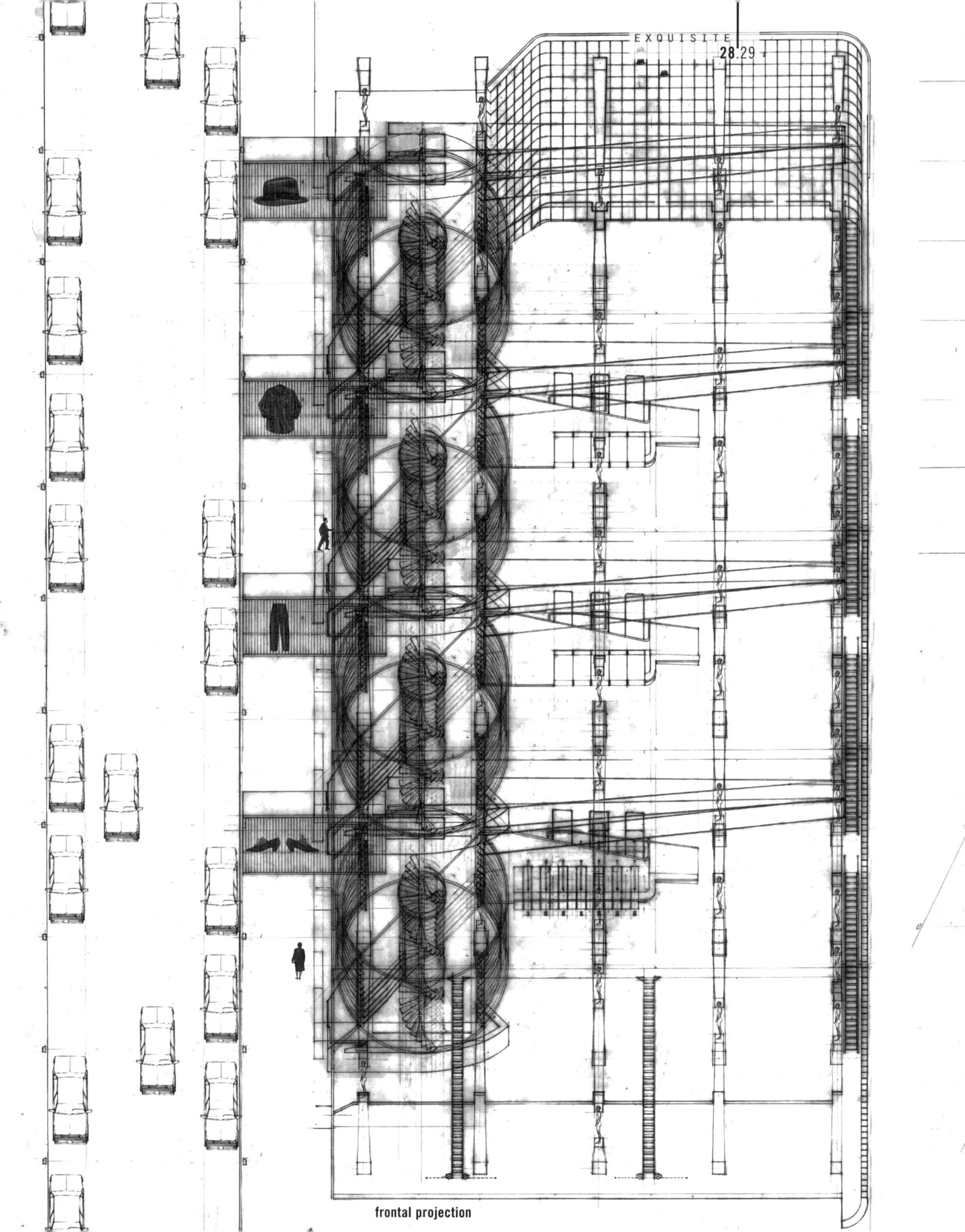

frontal projection

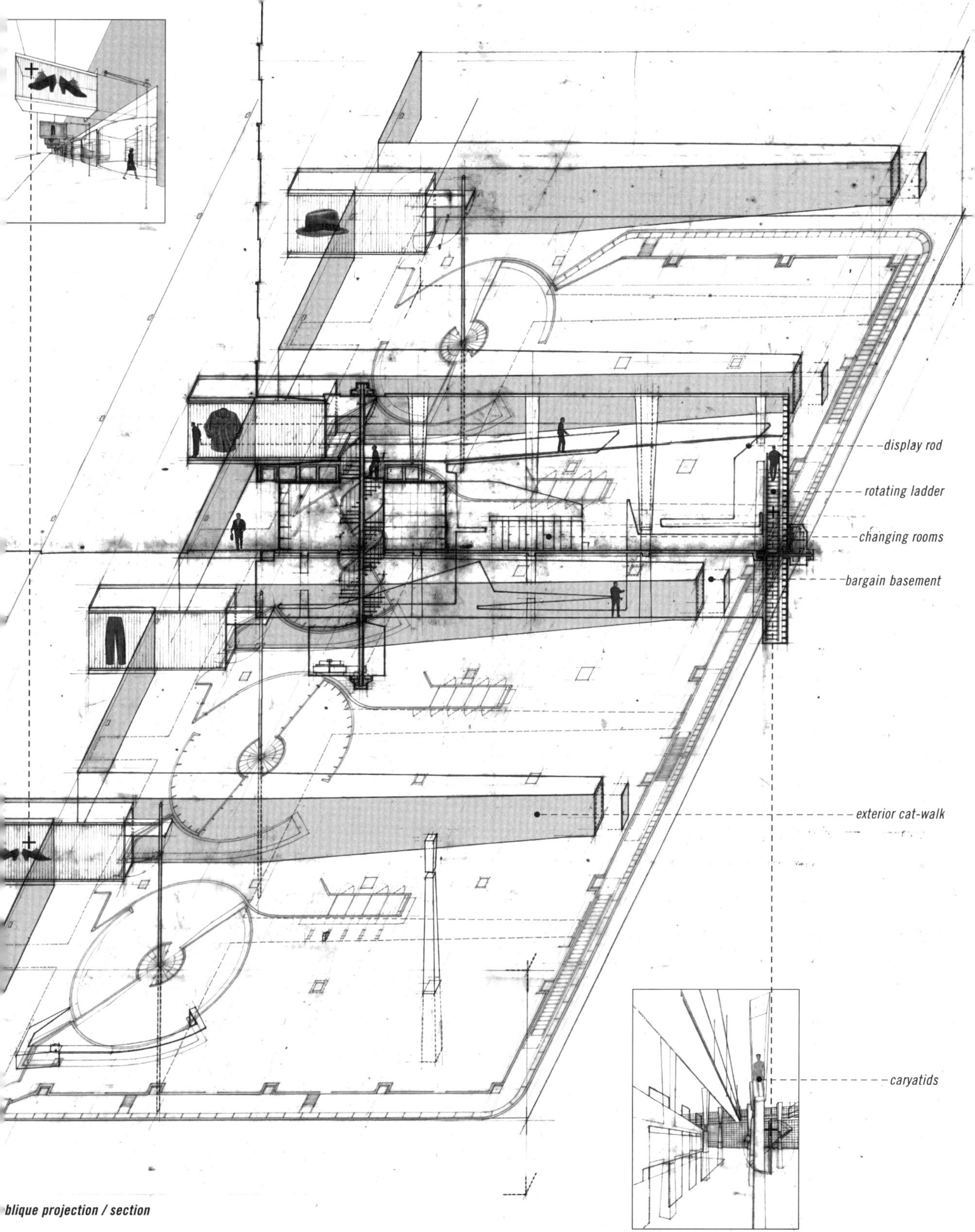

blique projection / section

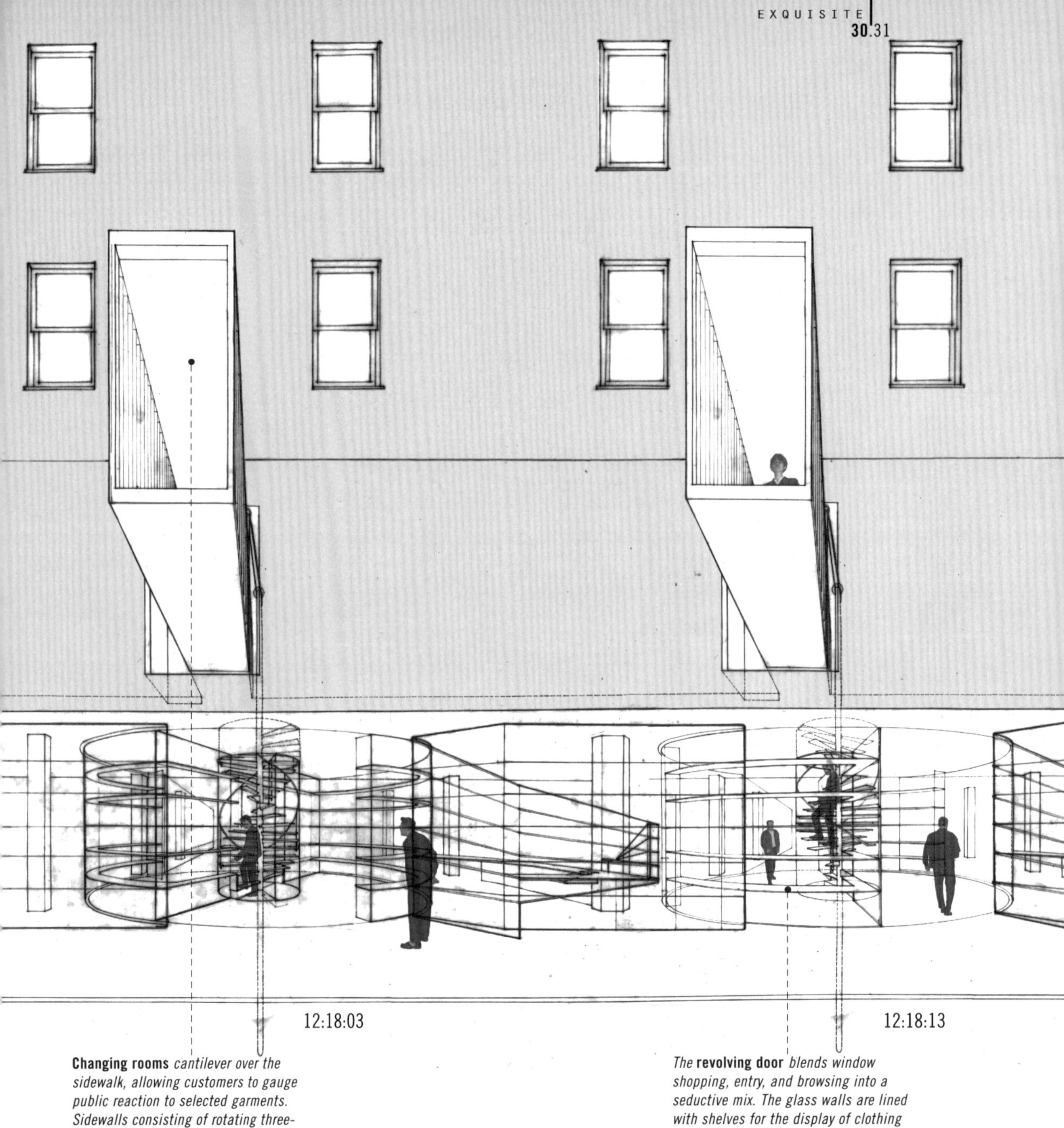

Changing rooms *cantilever over the sidewalk, allowing customers to gauge public reaction to selected garments. Sidewalls consisting of rotating three-sided signs alternate views of promenading patrons with advertising images of corresponding articles of clothing. These projecting runways act as an extrusion of the store interior into the public space of the street. Reversing this logic, catwalks within the store draw the outside into the heart of the store, allowing for the testing of outerwear in actual weather conditions.*

The **revolving door** *blends window shopping, entry, and browsing into a seductive mix. The glass walls are lined with shelves for the display of clothing in perpetual rotation. The motion of the door conspires with the desire produced by the object, drawing the distracted gaze of the passer-by and luring the pedestrian into the mobile space of the door. The conventional distinction between sidewalk and entry is blurred.*

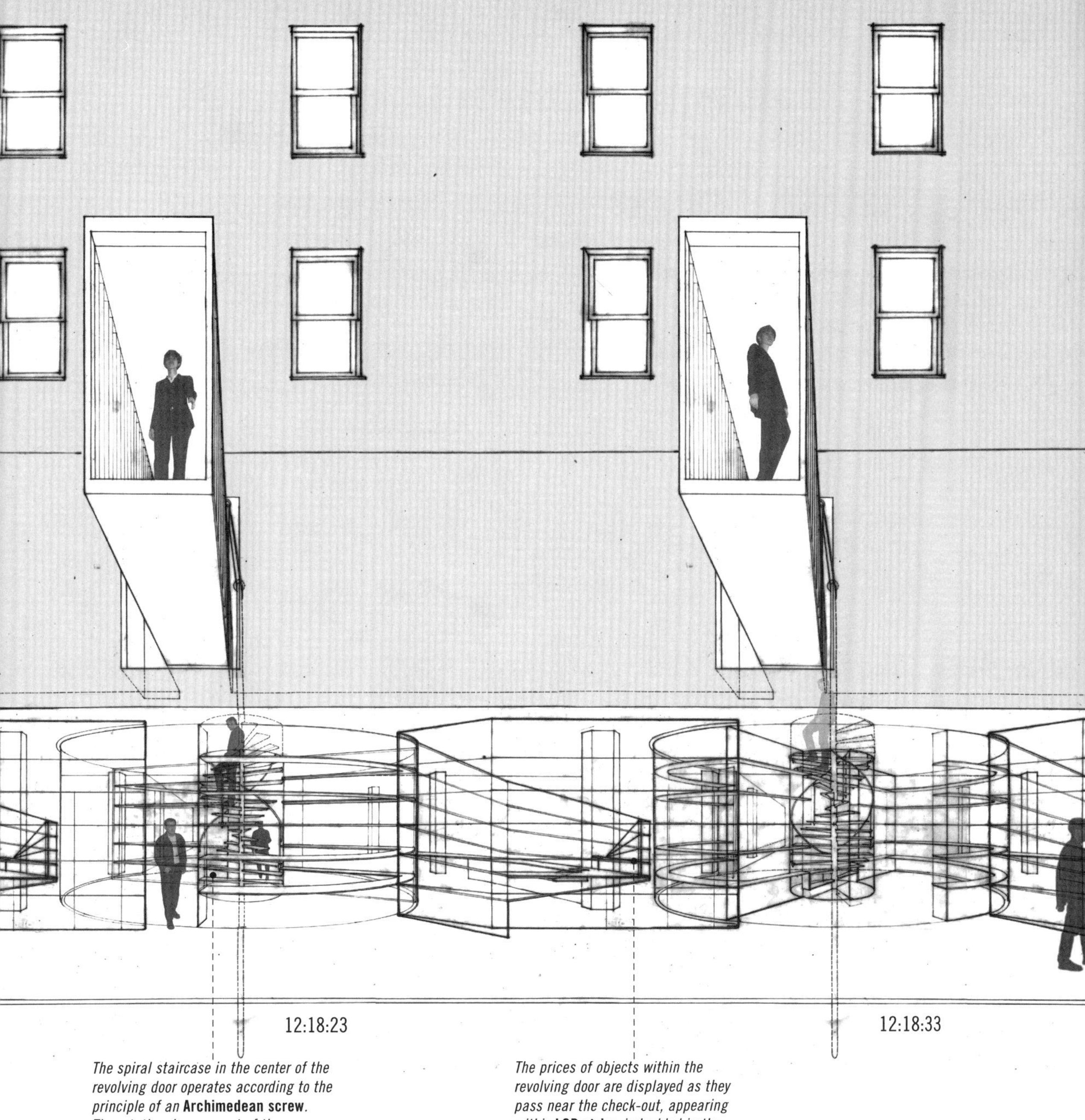

The spiral staircase in the center of the revolving door operates according to the principle of an **Archimedean screw***. The rotational movement of the staircase counteracts the forward motion of the body, allowing the user to ascend vertically while maintaining the same position in plan—one climbs the staircase while walking in place. The staircase's double helical structure facilitates unimpeded travel in both directions simultaneously.*

The prices of objects within the revolving door are displayed as they pass near the check-out, appearing within **LCD strips** *imbedded in the glass of the storefront wall.*

. elevators . security desks . front doors . parking spaces . loading docks . sidewalks . payphones . floor plates . lobbies . mailboxes . benches . potted plants . tax

This speculative urban prototype begins with the evacuation of the proprietary divisions between the multiple separate lobbies that comprise a single Manhattan block. The distinction between sidewalk and lobby is also erased, extending the space of the street to the elevator door and turning the street level of the block into a *free lobby*. As a space for chance meetings, detours, and deviations, this contiguous ground produces a blending of the multiple publics accessing the divergent programs above. A recombinant urban type is built upon the residual elevator cores and the inhabitable plenum above. The top surface of the plinth is developed as a patchwork of landscapes that registers the original divisions of the block.

free lobby . block 1290

site: **Manhattan Block 1290**

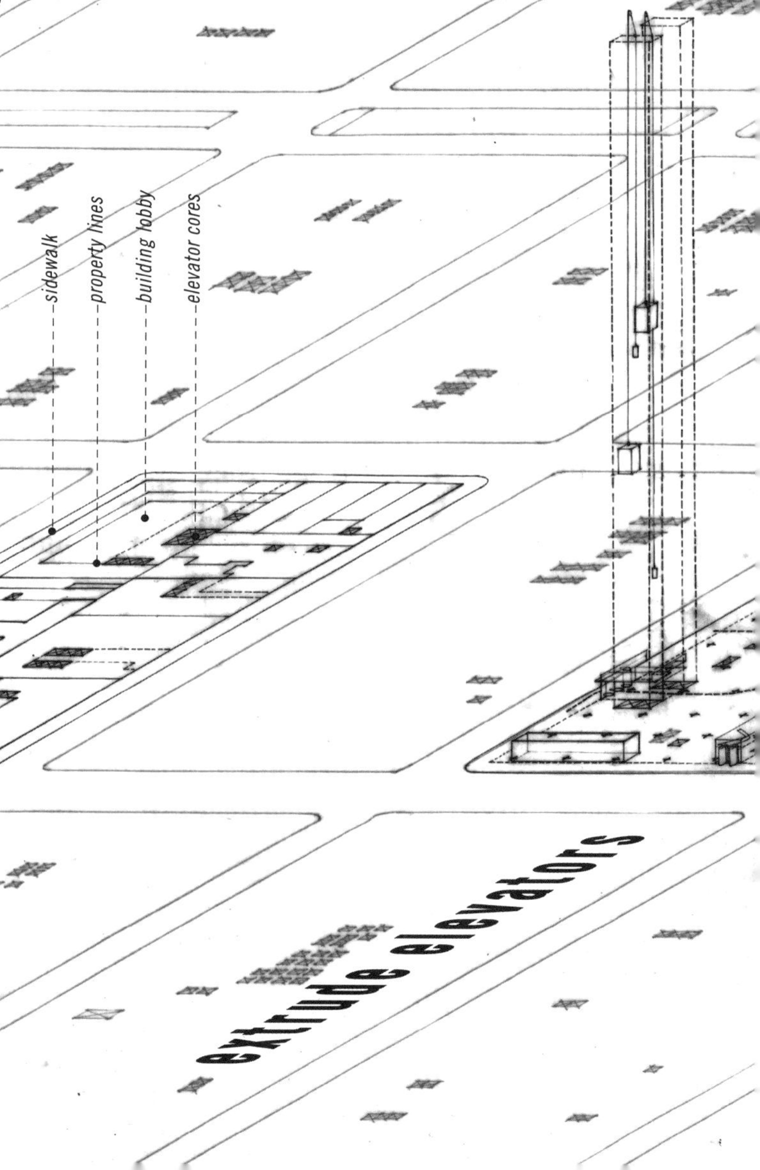

sidewalk
property lines
building lobby
elevator cores

evacuate

extrude elevators

towers
elevators
gardens
inhabitable plenum
residual entries
holdouts
car-ousels
reinhabit as free lobby

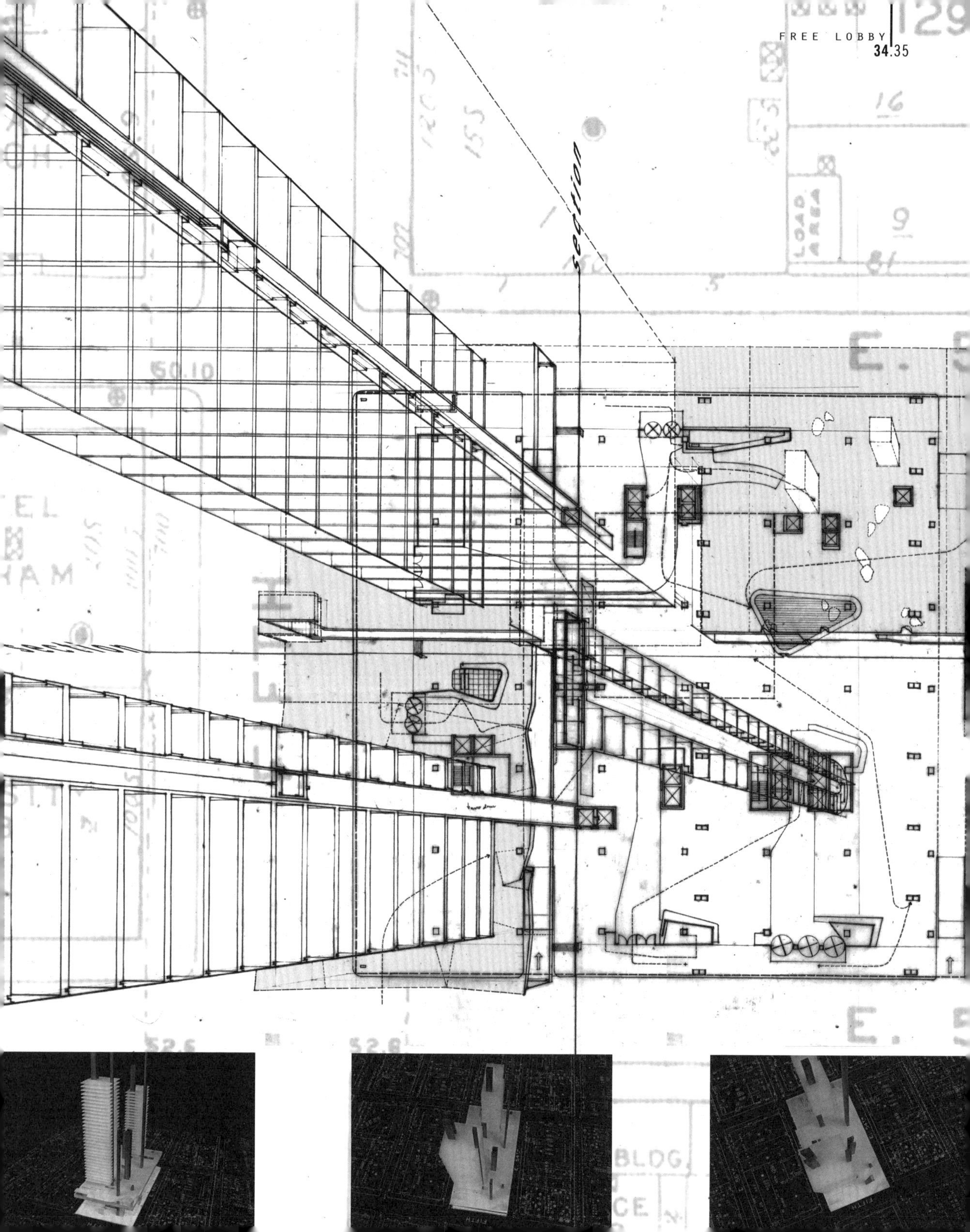
section

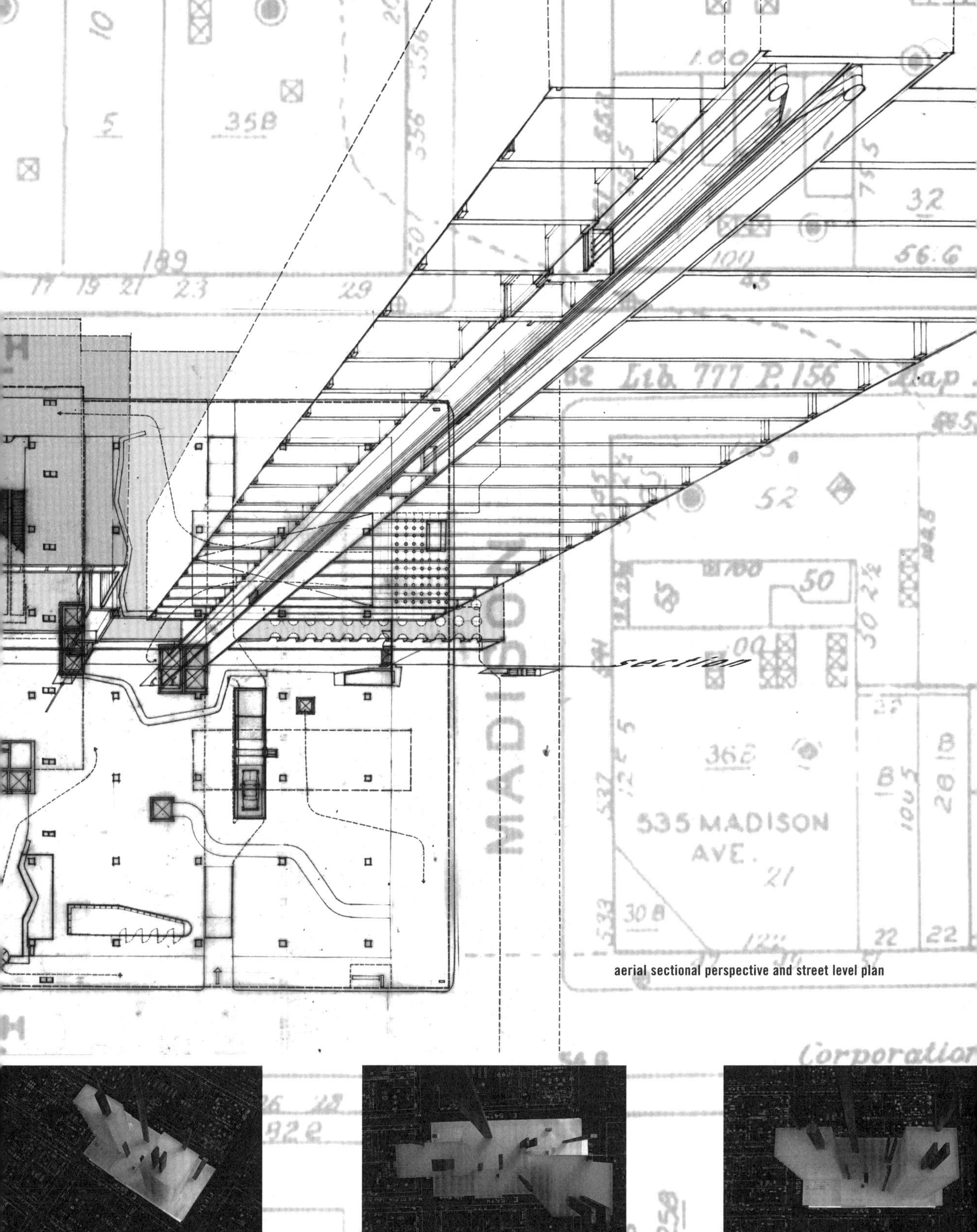

aerial sectional perspective and street level plan

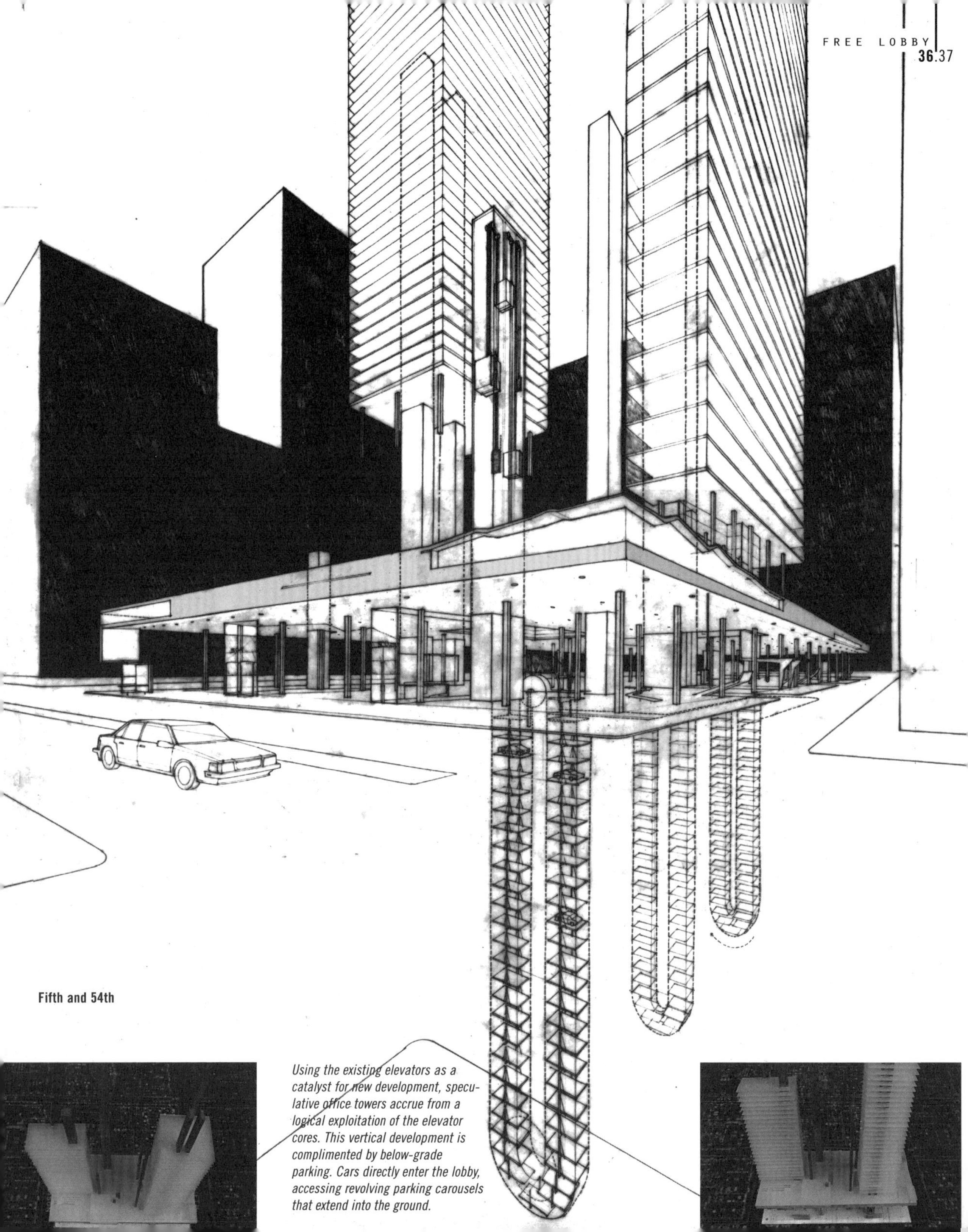

Fifth and 54th

Using the existing elevators as a catalyst for new development, speculative office towers accrue from a logical exploitation of the elevator cores. This vertical development is complimented by below-grade parking. Cars directly enter the lobby, accessing revolving parking carousels that extend into the ground.

Madison and 55th

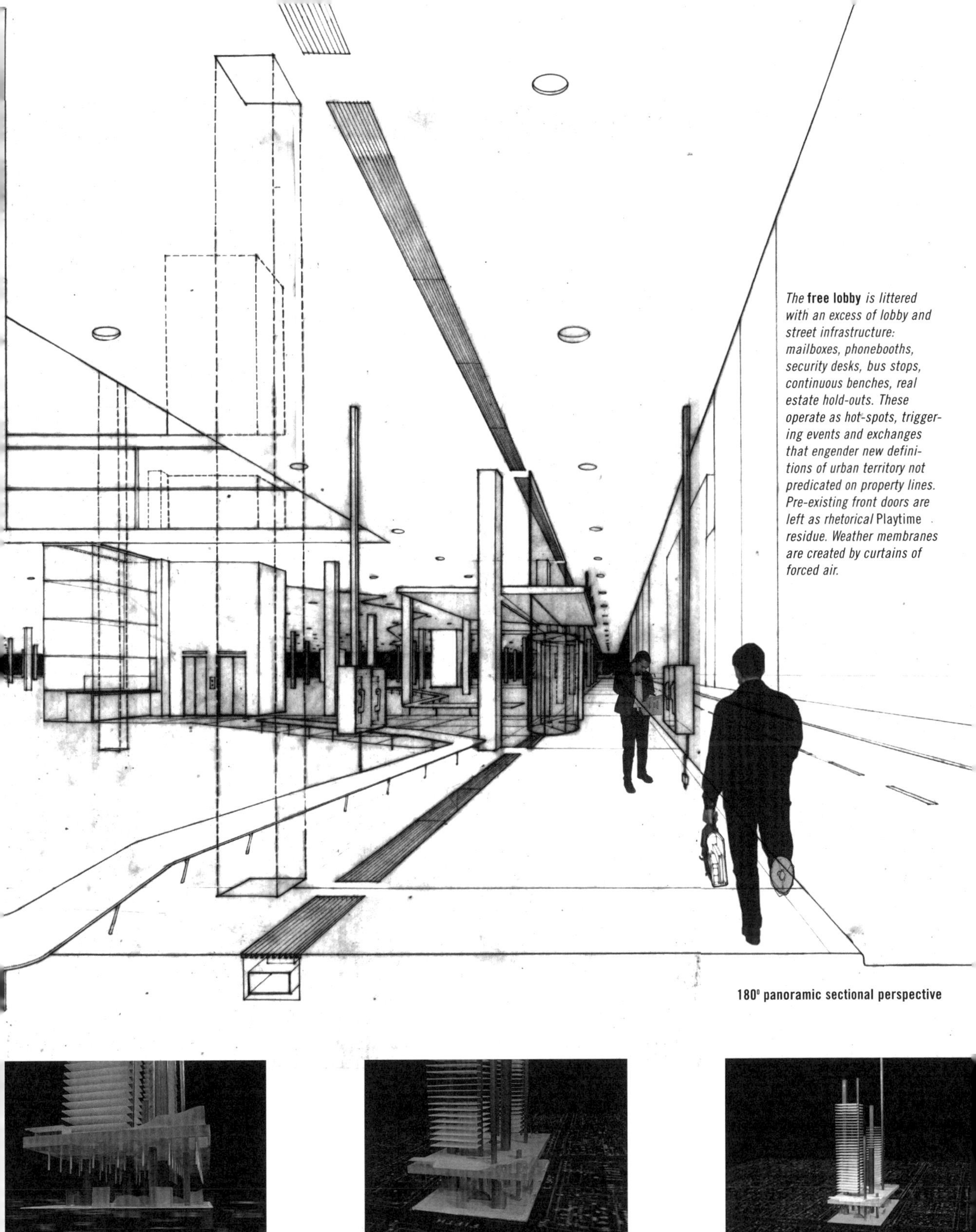

The **free lobby** *is littered with an excess of lobby and street infrastructure: mailboxes, phonebooths, security desks, bus stops, continuous benches, real estate hold-outs. These operate as hot-spots, triggering events and exchanges that engender new definitions of urban territory not predicated on property lines. Pre-existing front doors are left as rhetorical* Playtime *residue. Weather membranes are created by curtains of forced air.*

180° panoramic sectional perspective

. plazas . 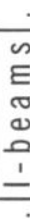 I-beams . offices . curtain walls . wheels . flag poles . high hats . window washers . ashtrays . smoking lounges . putting greens . brushes . sprinklers .

sketch: Chicago Historical Society

Mies's sketch of the plaza

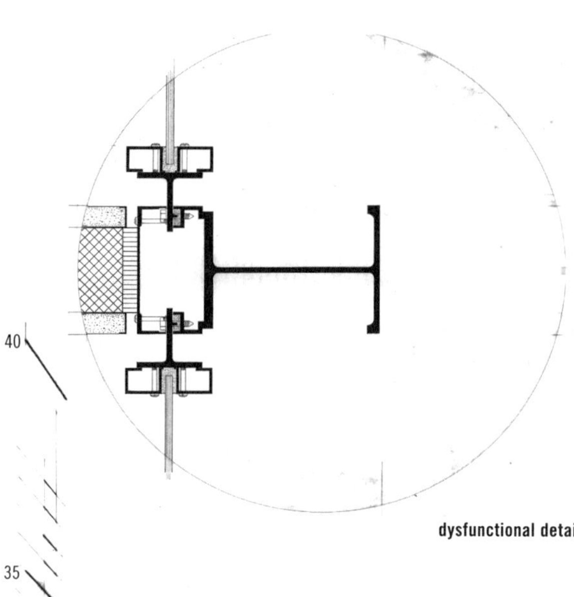
dysfunctional detail

This landscape supplement for the Seagram Building returns function to the two anomalous, nonfunctional aspects in Mies van der Rohe's New York masterpiece: the I-beams and the tree plaza. Mies-on-a-Beam (*mise-en-abyme*) transforms the ornamental curtain wall I-beams into wheel tracks for a pair of mobile grass platforms linked to the window washing hoist. The platforms rejuvenate the ineffective grove of trees at street level, in which the architect took great interest, by making them accessible to all floors of the building. With the foliage-enhanced plaza available at every level, Mies's desire for the absolute sameness of each floor is brought closer to fruition. In addition to cleaning the windows, the surface serves as a smoking terrace, an executive putting green, and a cantilevered roof, complete with high-hats underneath for outdoor illumination. Each detail is designed to do more with *less-is-more* through a doubling of function.

mies-on-a-beam

***site:* seagram building**

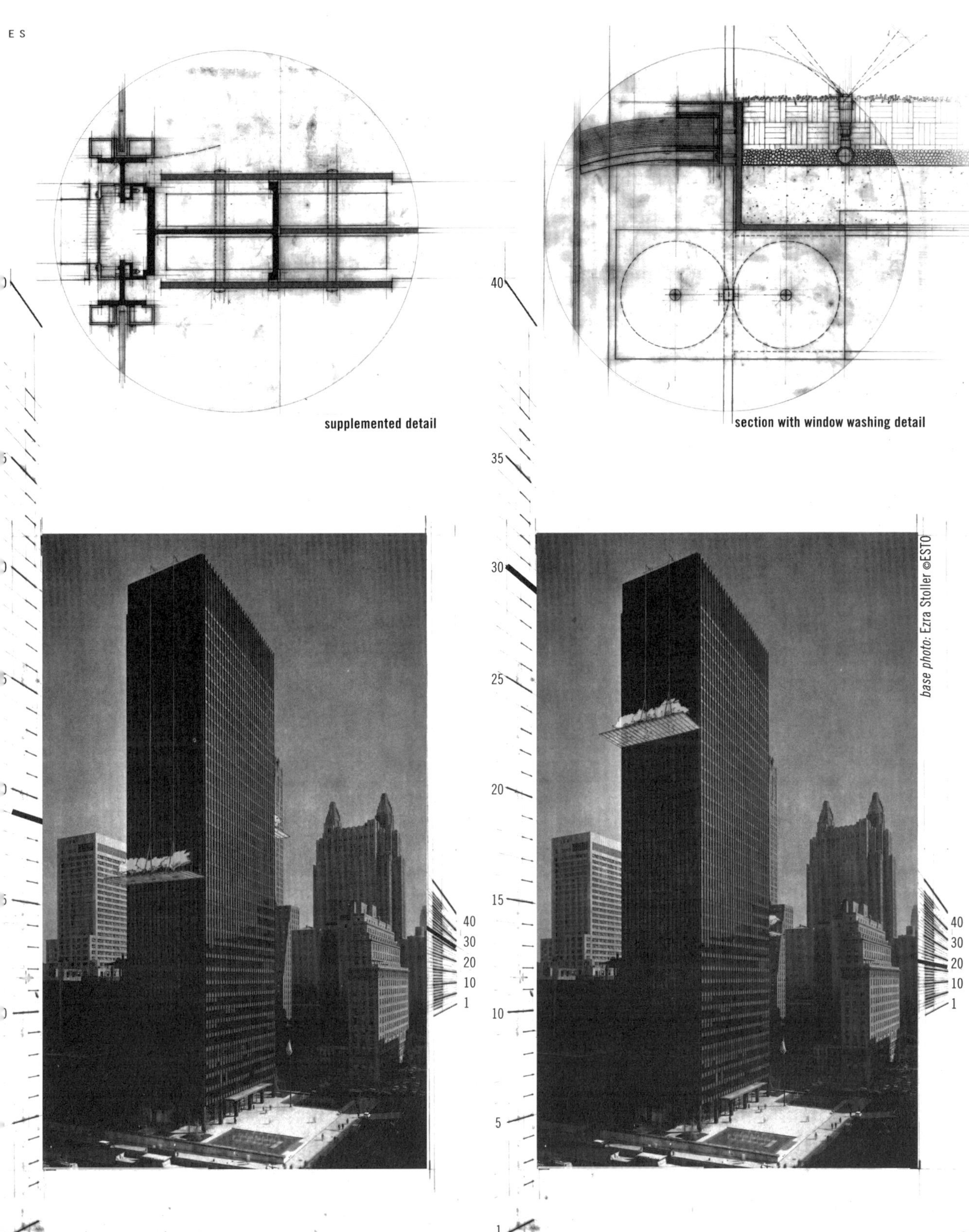

supplemented detail

section with window washing detail

base photo: Ezra Stoller ©ESTO

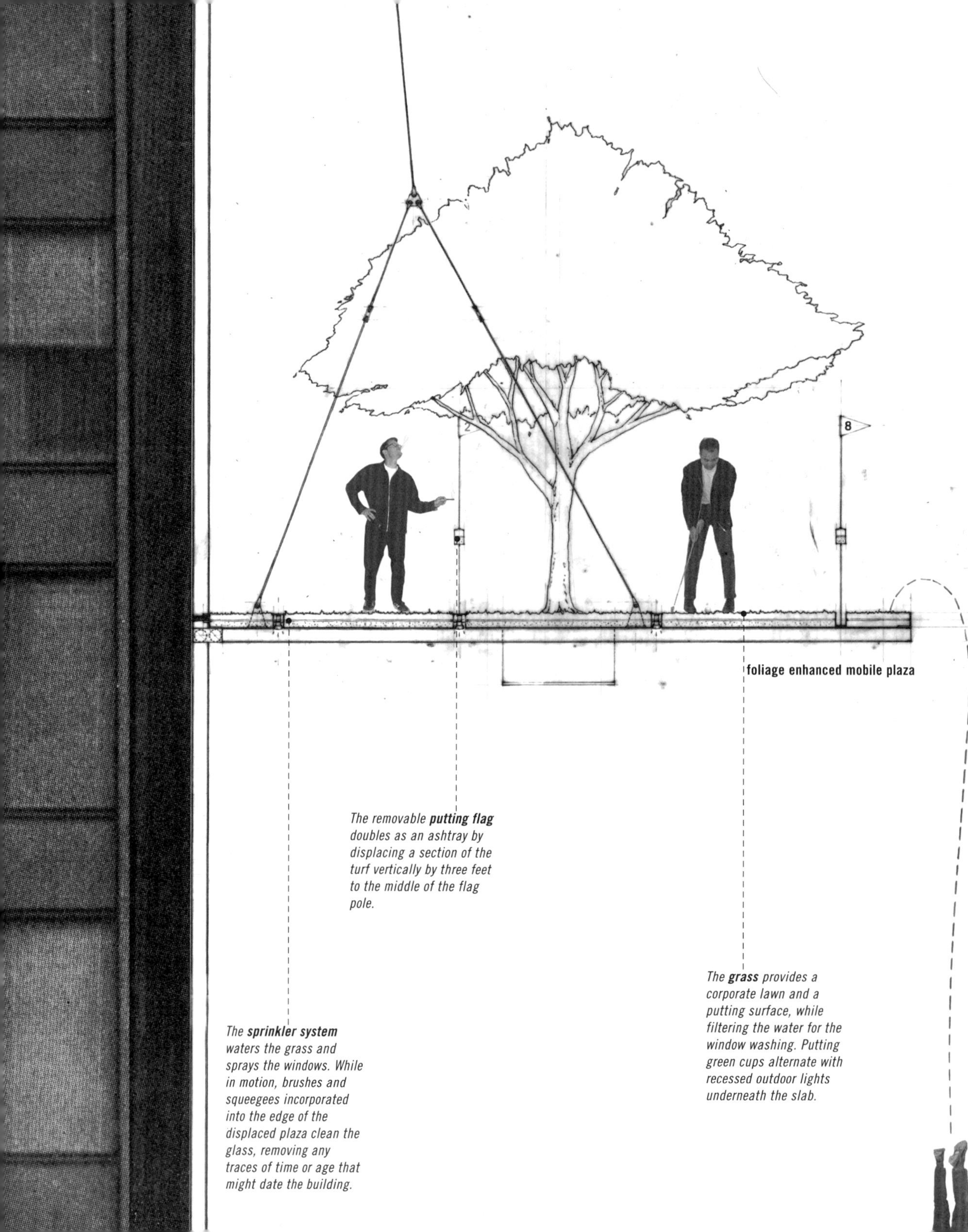
2
8
foliage enhanced mobile plaza
The removable **putting flag** doubles as an ashtray by displacing a section of the turf vertically by three feet to the middle of the flag pole.
The **grass** provides a corporate lawn and a putting surface, while filtering the water for the window washing. Putting green cups alternate with recessed outdoor lights underneath the slab.
The **sprinkler system** waters the grass and sprays the windows. While in motion, brushes and squeegees incorporated into the edge of the displaced plaza clean the glass, removing any traces of time or age that might date the building.

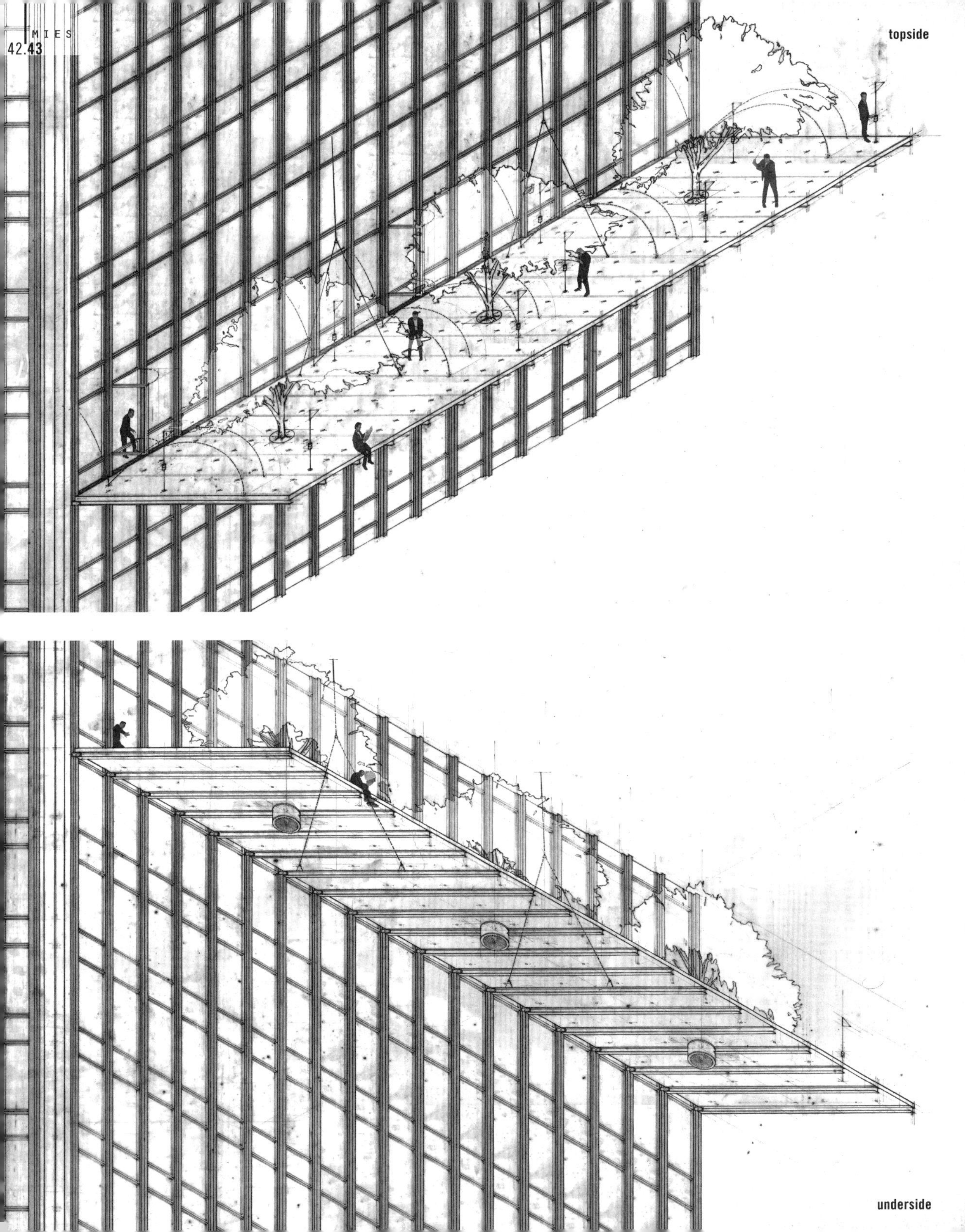
topside
underside

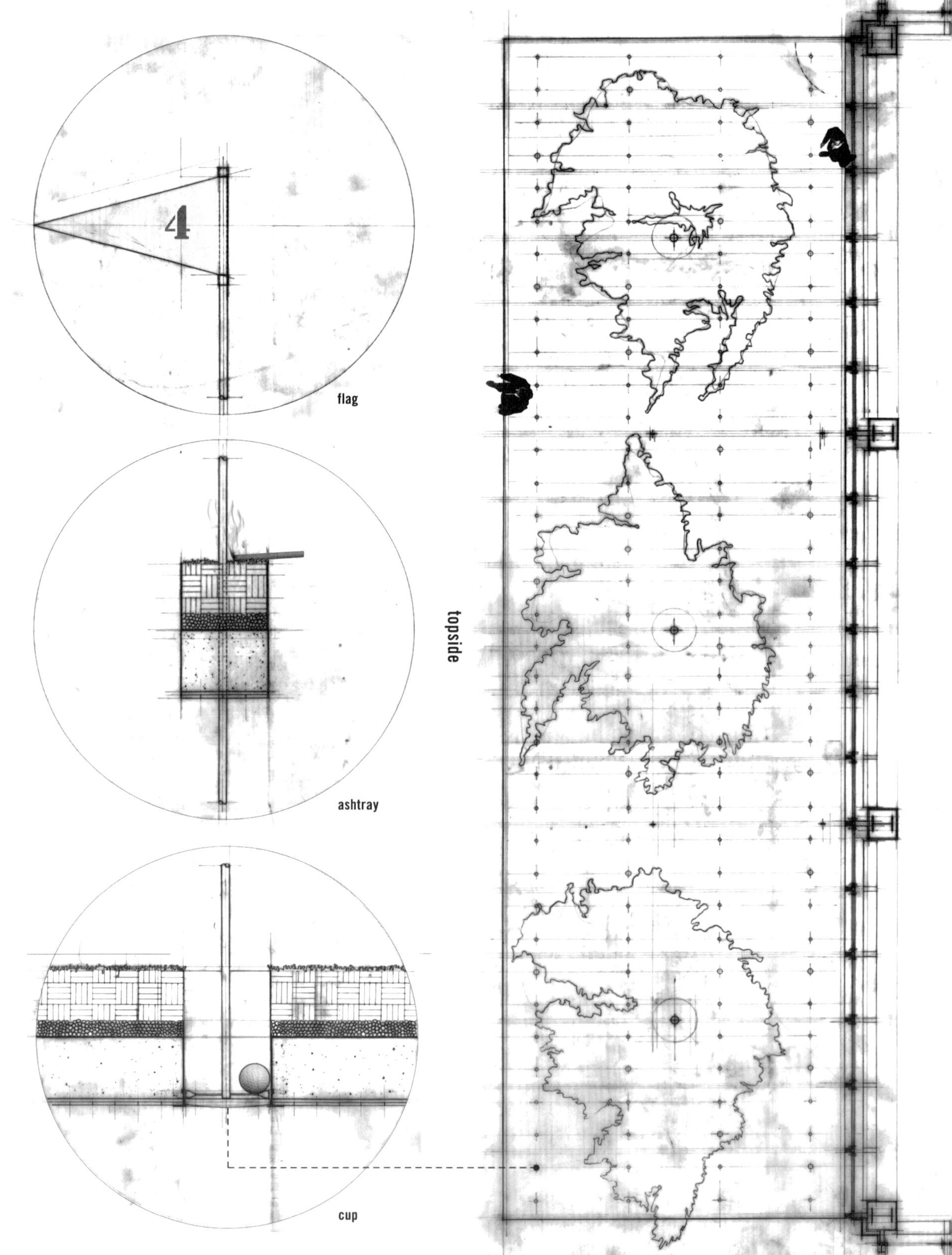

4
flag
ashtray
cup
topside

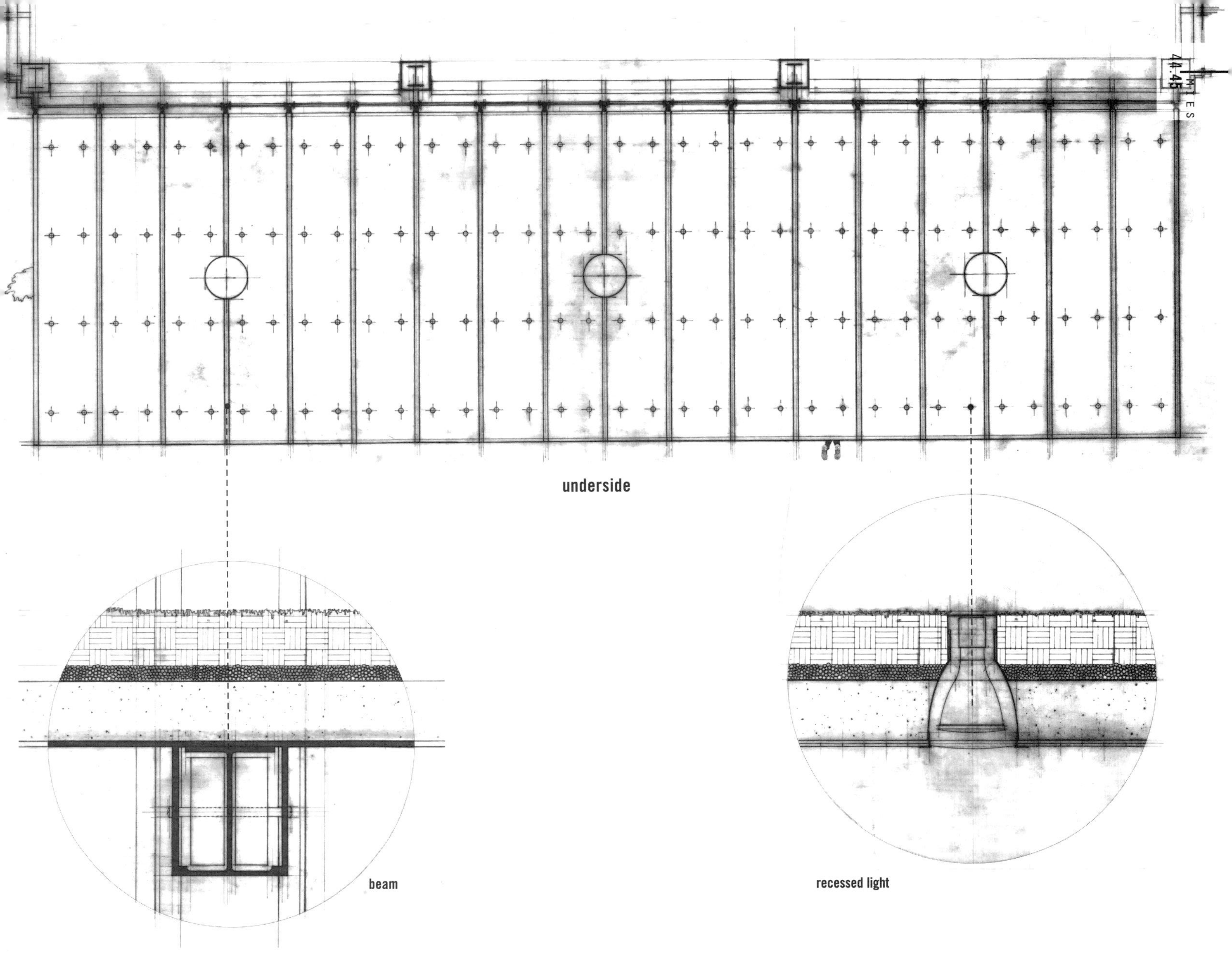
underside
beam
recessed light

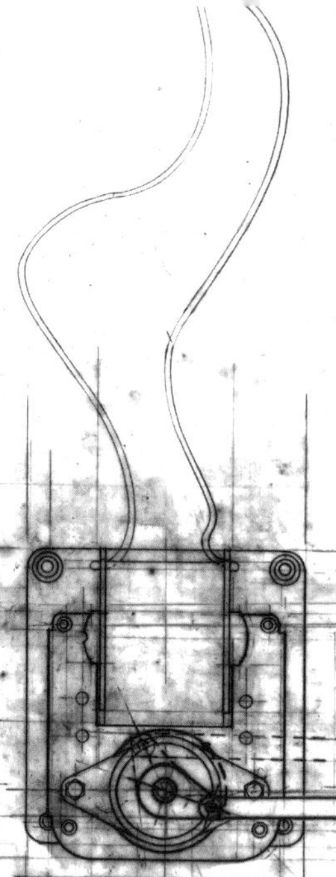

pull of beauty

site: **StoreFront for Art and Architecture**
collaborator: **Peter Pelsinski**

This exhibition required the display of 150 pieces of architectural hardware (doorknobs, knockers, drawer pulls, etc.), including commissioned, historic, and generic pieces. The aim of the installation was to situate all of these items in a recognizable yet estranged relationship to their intended use. The display negotiated between the objects reading as functional artifacts on the one hand and as purely formal objects on the other. Through its engagement with the viewer's body, the display established a fluctuating condition in which the assembled pieces alternated between utilitarian and aesthetic readings. A continuous wall composed of a series of conventional doors arranged in a line and supported from aluminum struts split the already constricted space of the gallery down its center. This created a tension between the wall's role as an object for display and the conventional function of the door as a means of passage from one space to another.

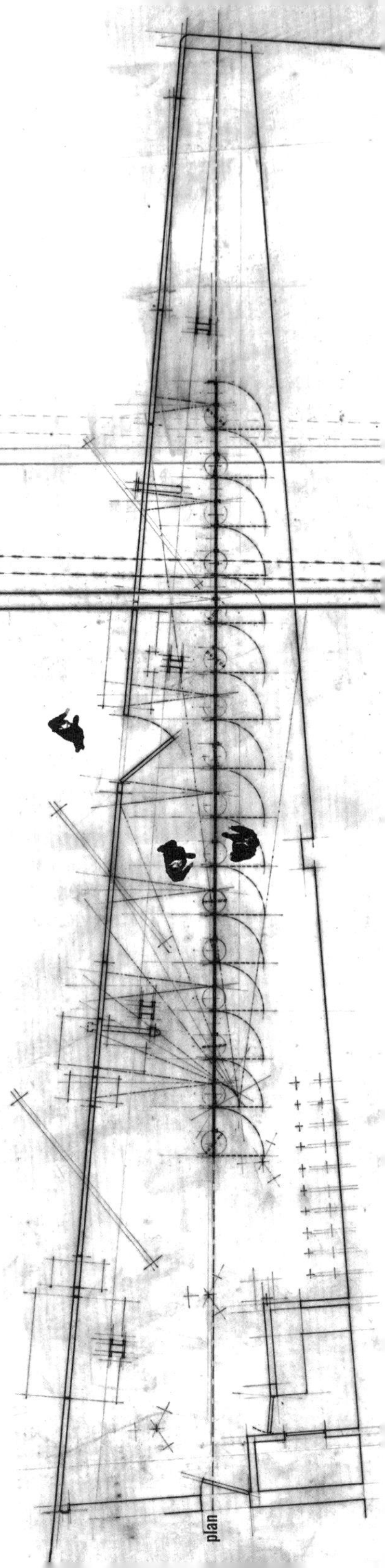

plan

mechanized model
back
front

The hardware enticed one to physically engage with the exhibition, breaking down the prohibition against physical contact in a gallery space. Hardware was arranged on the doors in such a way that it referred to its conventional use and position; however, a series of secondary operations acted to estrange the expected relationship between the body and the various kinds of exhibited hardware.

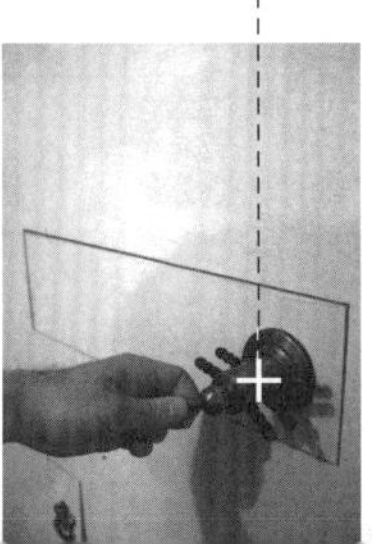

***Pivoting panels** switched knobs from the functional position at the side of the door to the dysfunctional position at the center. By rotating panels 180 degrees, access to hardware displayed on the opposite side of the wall was possible without actually passing through the door.*

The doors were elevated off the ground, displacing ***doorknobs*** *from their expected location to a height closer to the viewer's eye level. Operation of the knobs in some cases opened doors but in others only revealed additional hardware or the name of the artist or manufacturer—a means to access information rather than space.*

Each door incorporated a ***drawer*** *into its surface that was rotated vertically to deny function. Closing the drawer on one side of the gallery opened it on the other.*

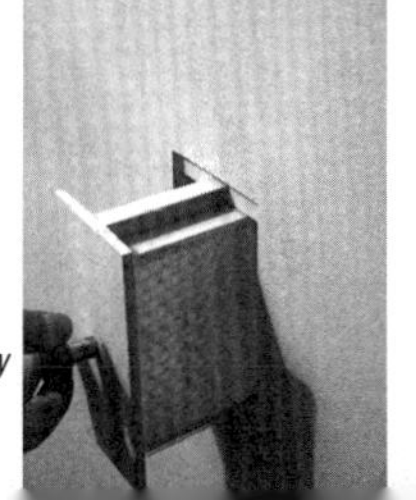

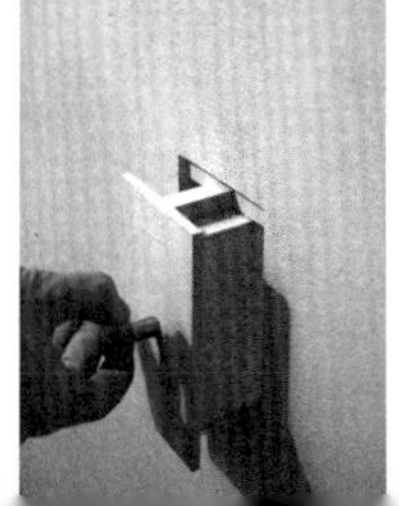

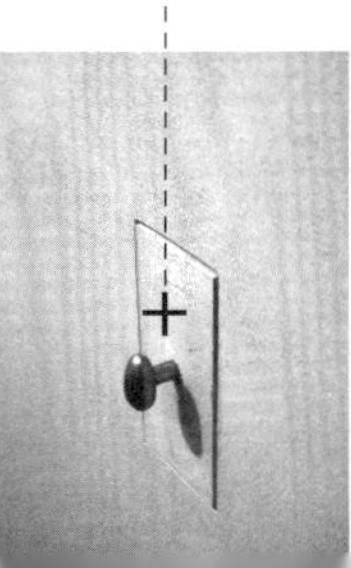

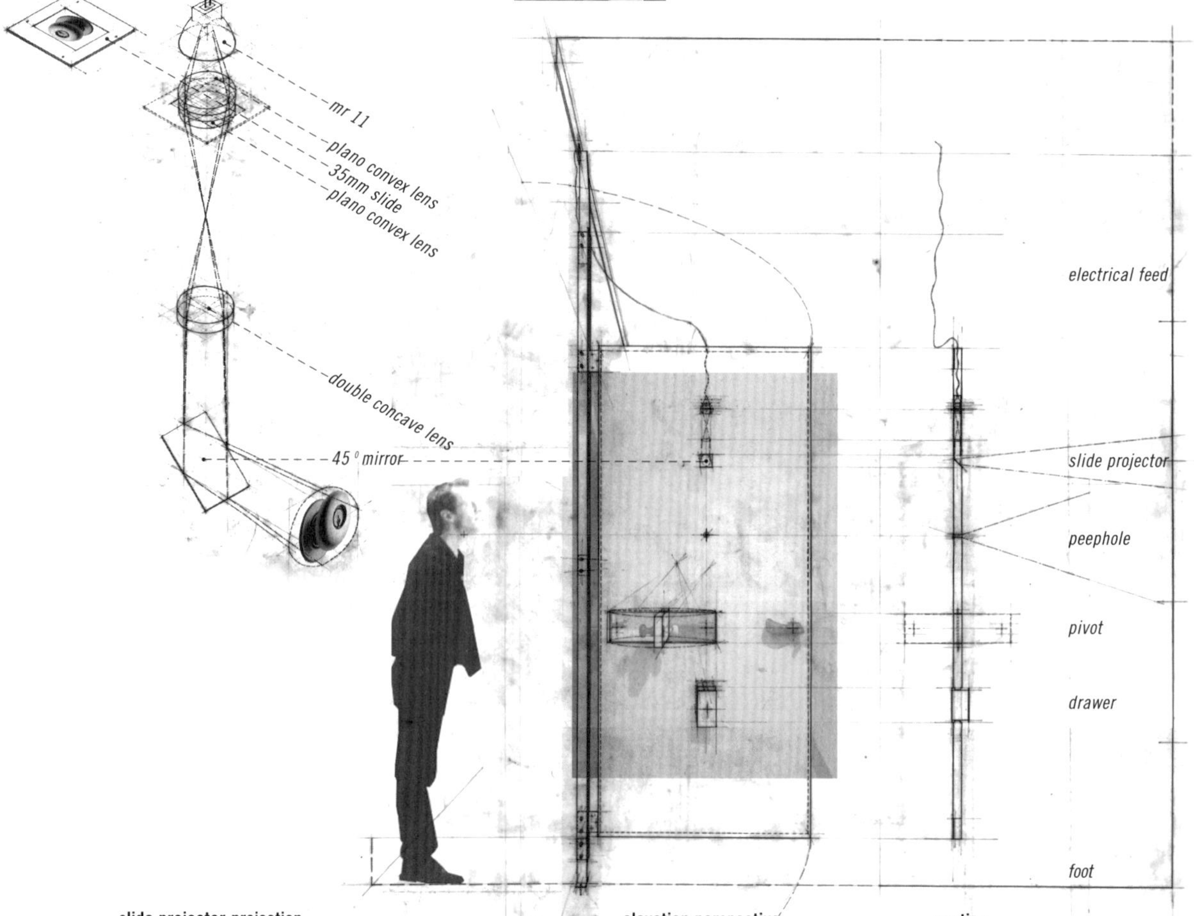

slide projector projection

elevation perspective

section

Peepholes *or* ***slide projectors*** *were embedded within the hollow doors. The custom made projectors cast images of historical hardware onto the adjacent gallery wall. Silk-screened directly onto the wall surface was a grid of engravings of ornaments that corresponded to the projected images. This created a matrix in which information itself was transformed into a decorative pattern. Opening the door anamophically distorted and displaced the projected image down the gallery wall.*

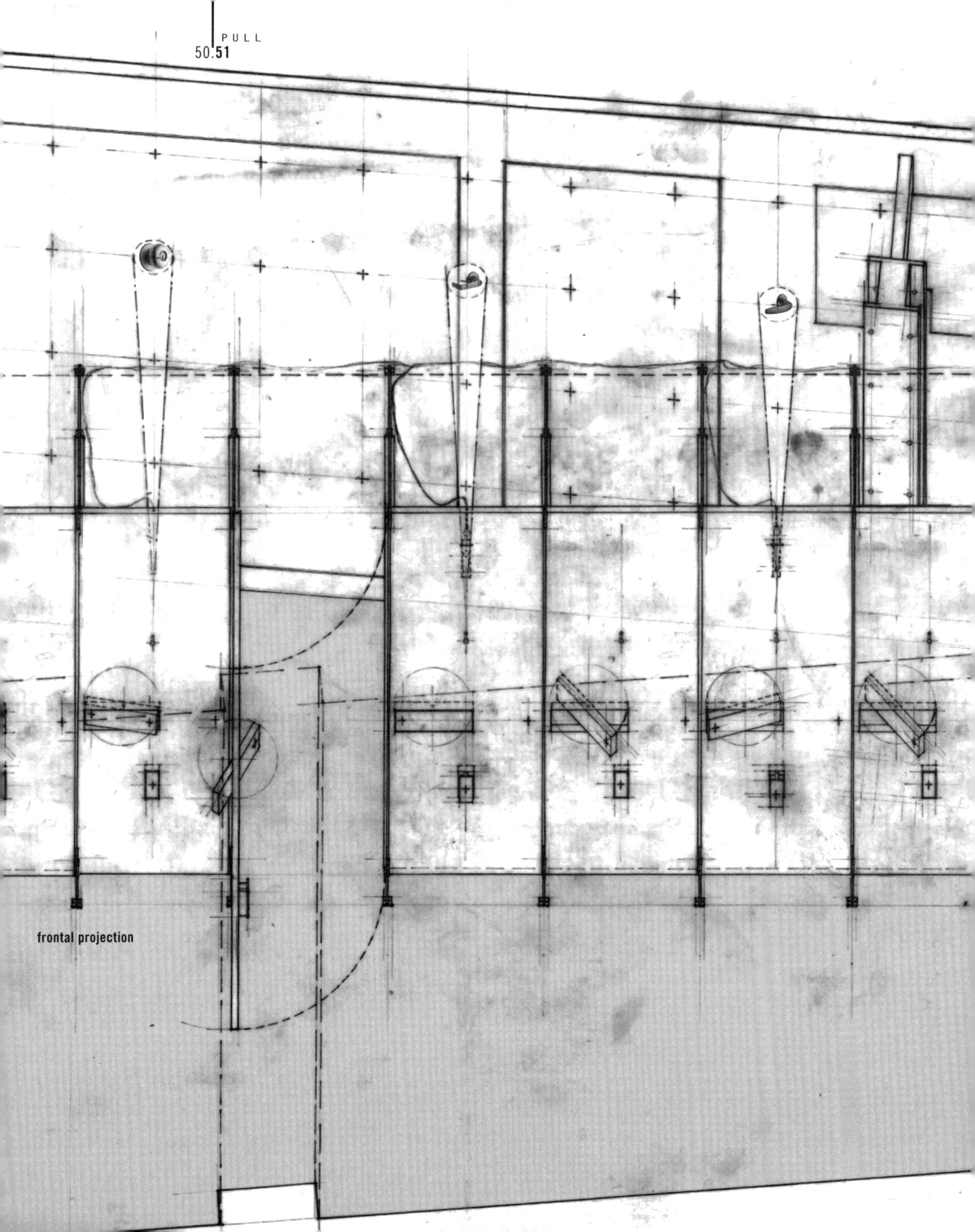

frontal projection

Previously a military base, Governers Island is located off the tip of Manhattan. As a potential addition of land to New York City, the large size of the island is just one link in the dialectic exchange between landfill and skyfill, the driving force transforming the lower end of Manhattan and its harbor. Every skyscraper erected requires a substantial excavation of earth that is then used to extend Manhattan through landfill. New skyscrapers can then be built upon this new land, and the cycle continues. This hypothetical proposal—the displacement of one of the Twin Towers of the World Trade Center to Governors Island—contests this dialectic. In a harbor filled with vertical monuments, the relocated twin is a horizontal monument. It marks the dividing line between the original land and recent landfill extension of the island. The tower is reconfigured as a horizontal housing, commercial, and office project, subverting the assumptions of vertical skyfill. What was once used vertically is reworked according to a new horizontal orientation—section becomes plan, floors become walls, vertical windows become the world's longest strip window, passenger elevators become people movers, and ceiling plenums become wall fixtures.

skyfill . landfill

***site:* Governors Island**

The appropriated condition of Manhattan at the moment of European horizontal expansion produces the desire for...

given

...the vertical production of skyfill at the end of Manhattan, demanding...

skyfill

...the passage of the Brooklyn-Battery Tunnel, horizontally linking Manhattan and Brooklyn, whose displaced earth doubles the size of Governors Island, and whose location makes economically possible...

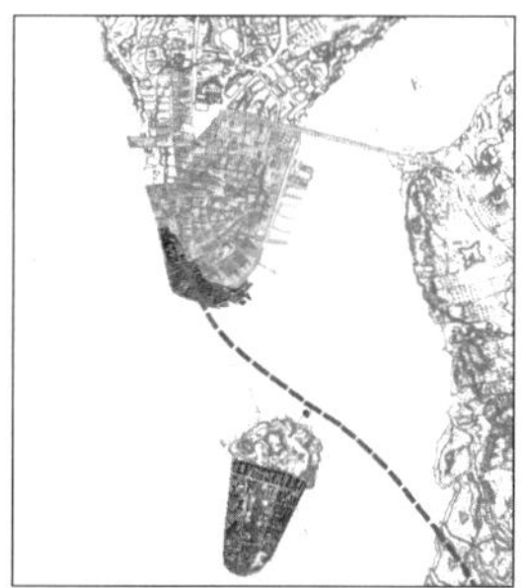

landfill

...the creation of the most egregious concatenation of skyfill and landfill, the Twin Towers, whose foundation excavations spread Manhattan into the Hudson River, leading to Battery Park City, a city within a city, a tabula rasa *ripe for more skyfill or...*

skyfill + landfill

104 103 102 101 100 99

...the reversal of the dialectic: skyfill/landfill. The de-twinning of Manhattan.

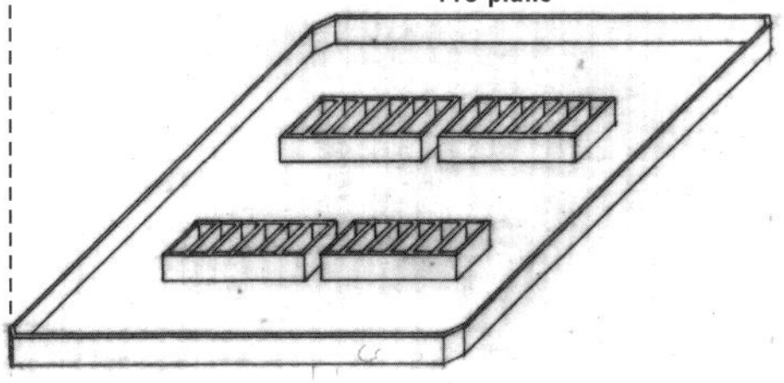

110 plans

skyfill

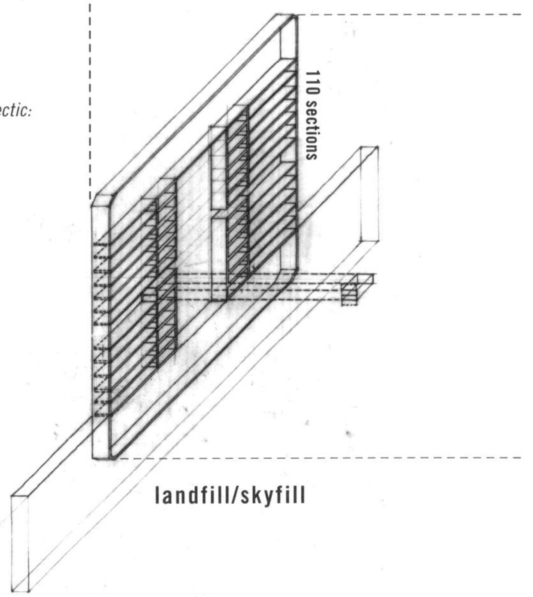

110 sections

landfill/skyfill

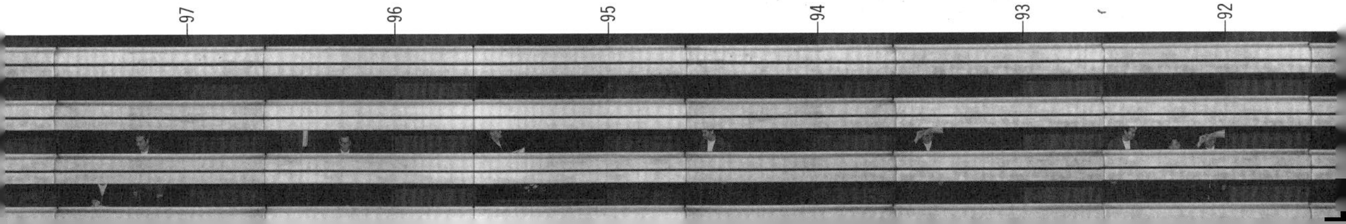

97 96 95 94 93 92

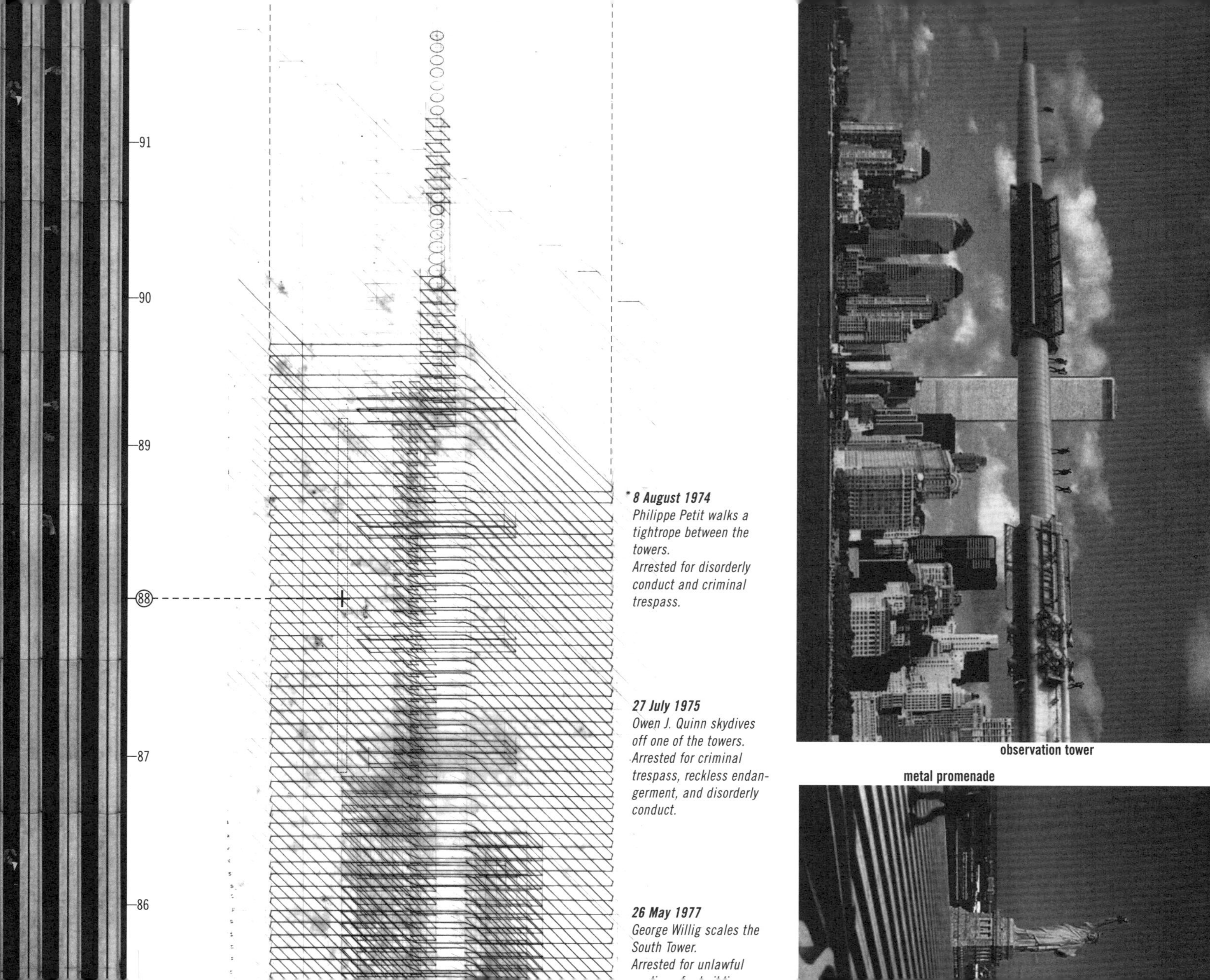

8 August 1974
Philippe Petit walks a tightrope between the towers.
Arrested for disorderly conduct and criminal trespass.

27 July 1975
Owen J. Quinn skydives off one of the towers.
Arrested for criminal trespass, reckless endangerment, and disorderly conduct.

26 May 1977
George Willig scales the South Tower.
Arrested for unlawful

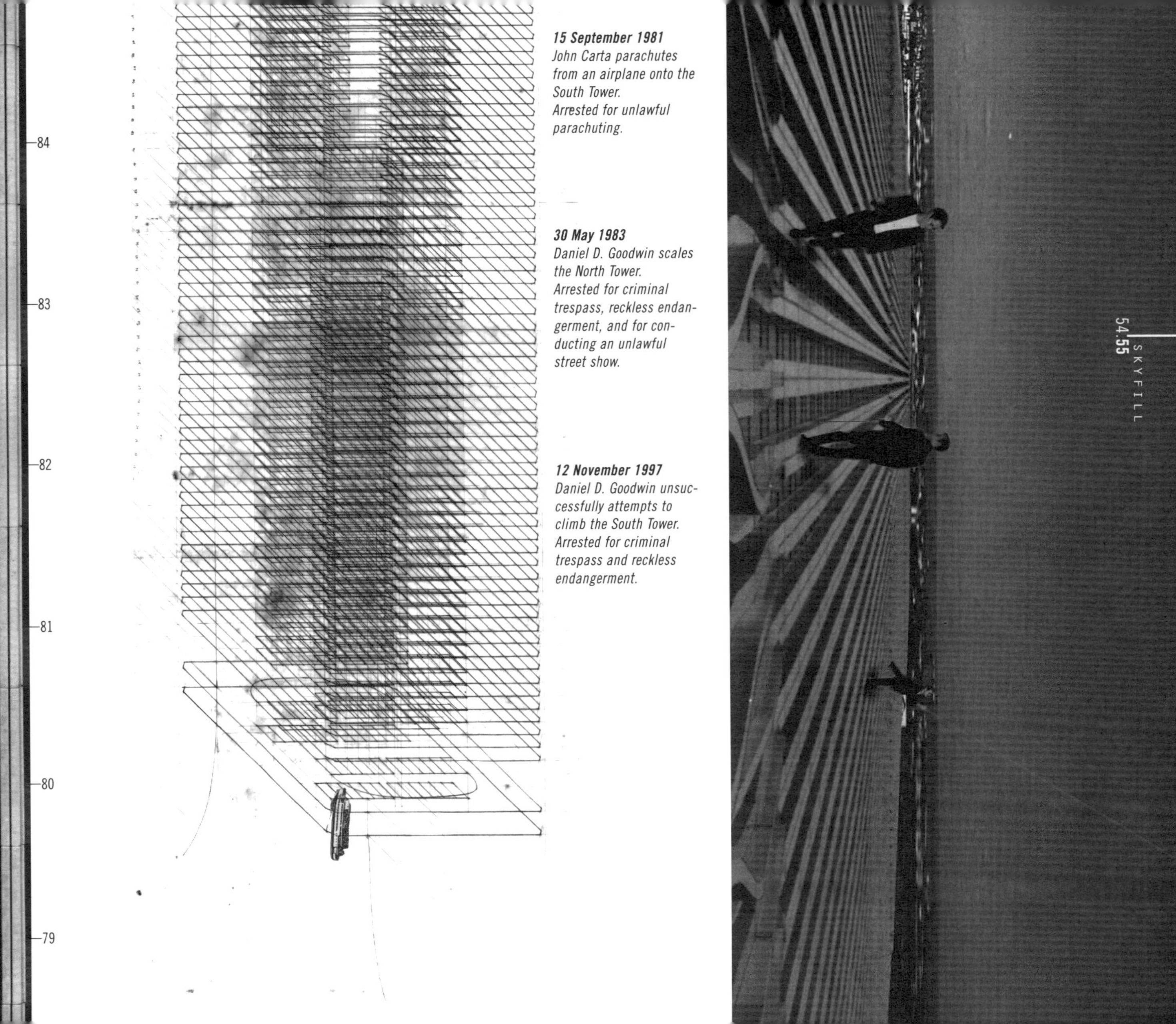

15 September 1981
John Carta parachutes from an airplane onto the South Tower.
Arrested for unlawful parachuting.

30 May 1983
Daniel D. Goodwin scales the North Tower.
Arrested for criminal trespass, reckless endangerment, and for conducting an unlawful street show.

12 November 1997
Daniel D. Goodwin unsuccessfully attempts to climb the South Tower.
Arrested for criminal trespass and reckless endangerment.

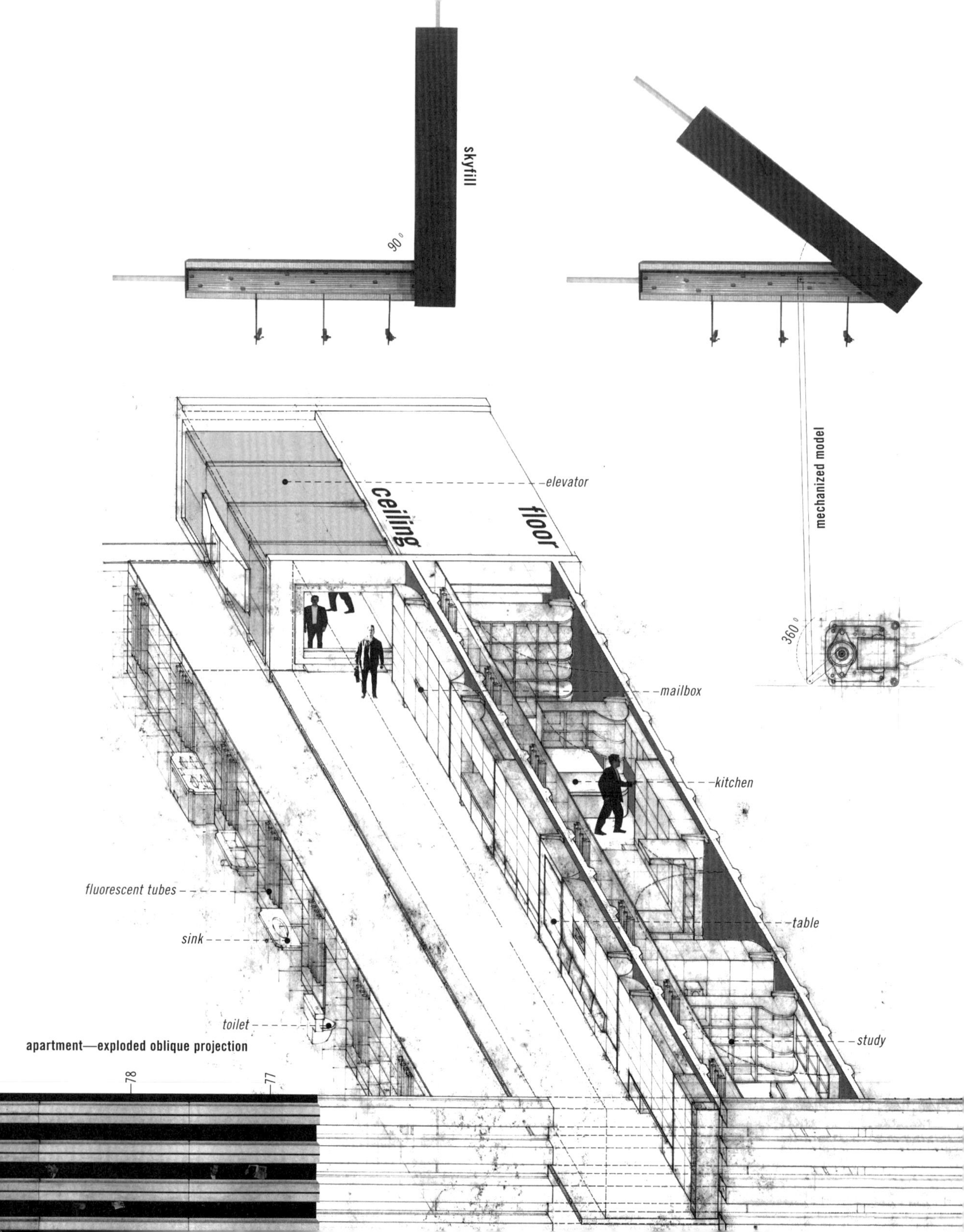

apartment—exploded oblique projection

landfill

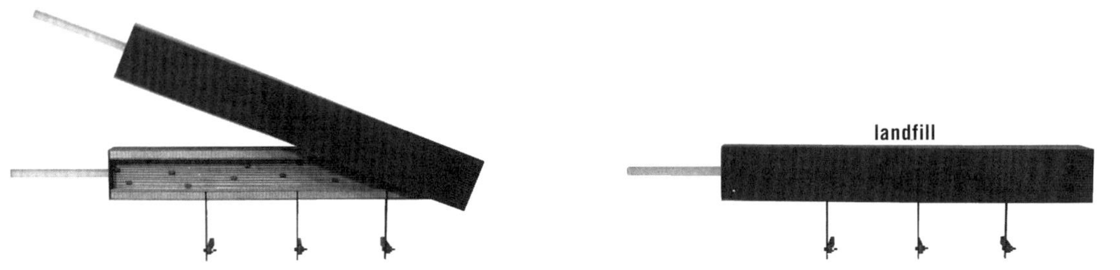

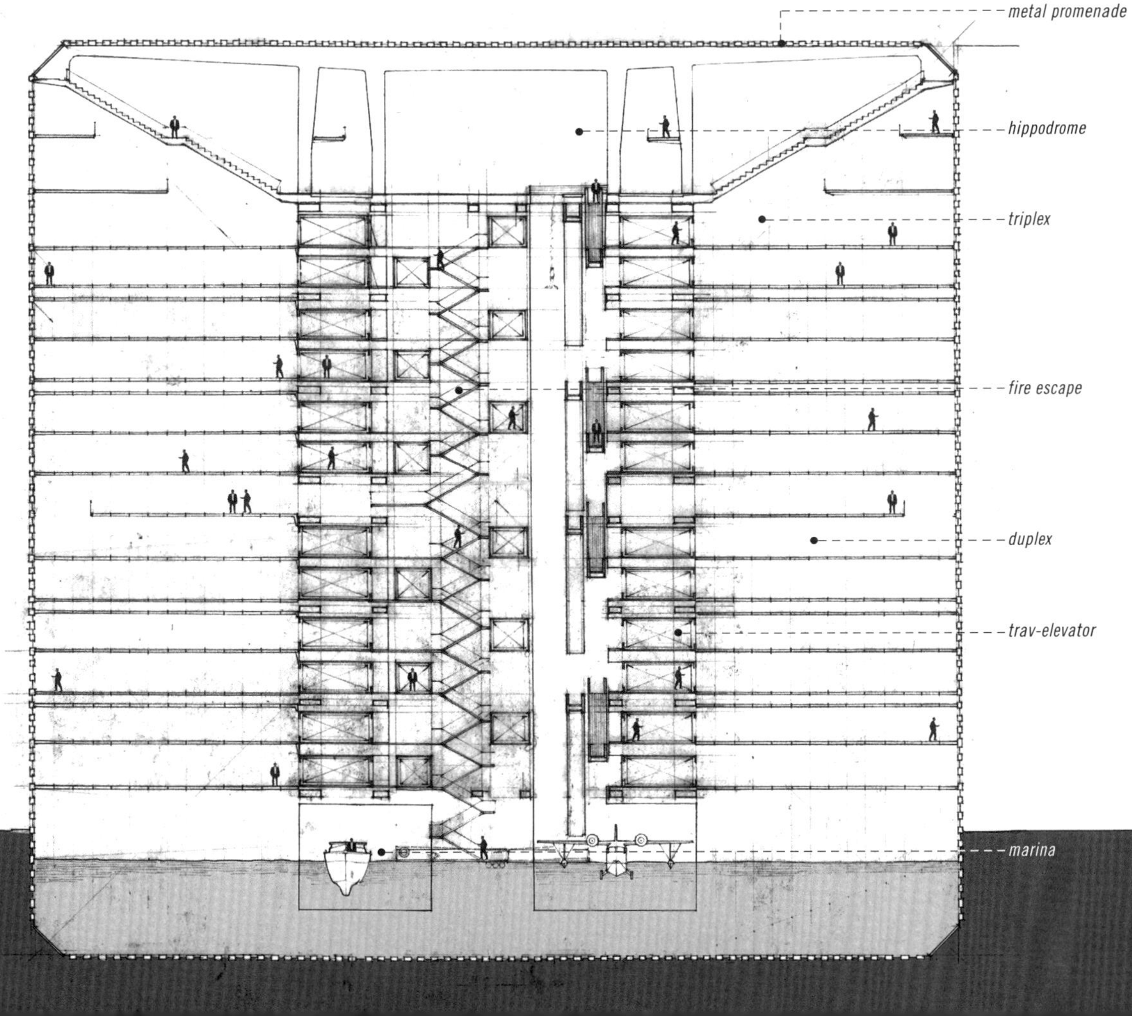
metal promenade
hippodrome
triplex
fire escape
duplex
trav-elevator
marina

section

What if typical gallery furniture was covertly used to inspect the spatial distinctions created by a floor? In this installation, three stools, a bookshelf, and a table were designed to tactically engage the presence of the basement located under a portion of the first floor gallery. The basement slips to the gallery as the gallery leaks to the basement, undermining the binary of the public, clean gallery and the private, dirty basement produced by the floor. By suspending the conventional gallery furniture

slip space

site: **StoreFront for Art and Architecture**
collaborator: **Peter Pelsinski**

between these two adjacent spaces, the floor is rendered a site of exchange. Presumed stability is questioned through the registration of fluctuations and slippages. Exchanges between the spaces rely on physical, tactile, and corporeal experiences rather than strictly visual ones.

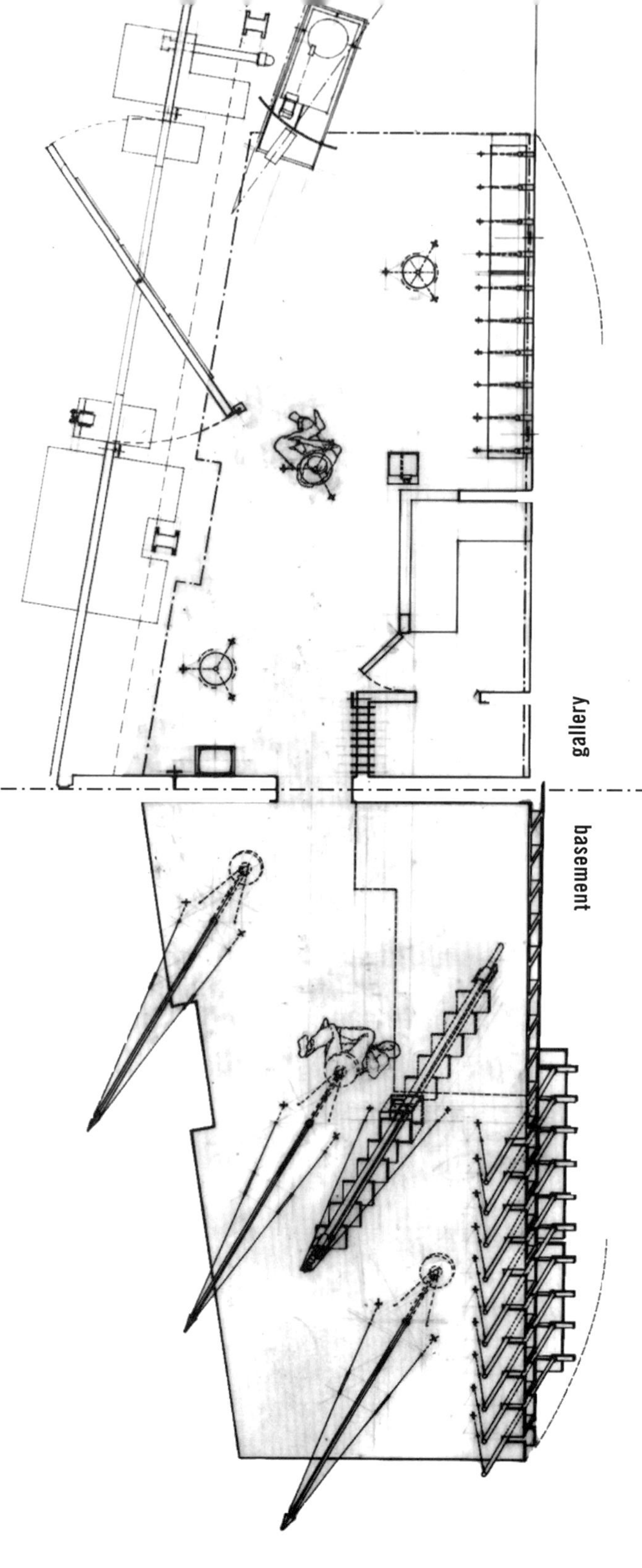

gallery

basement

gallery

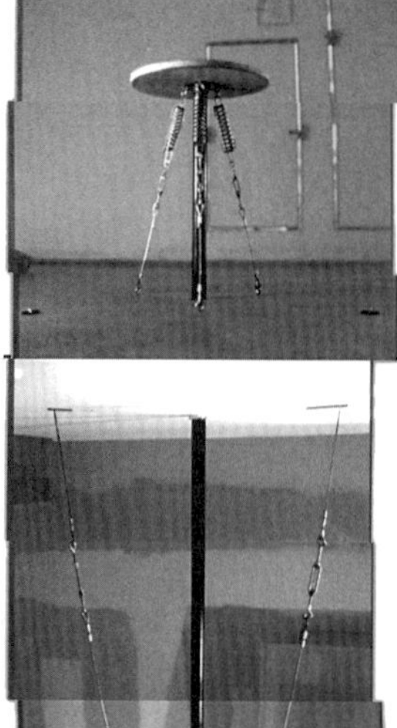
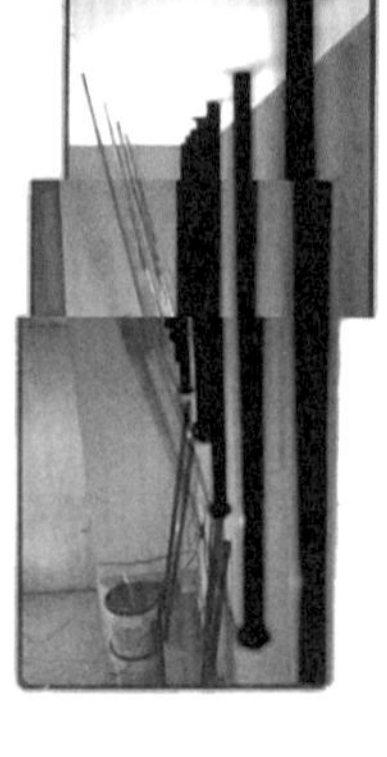

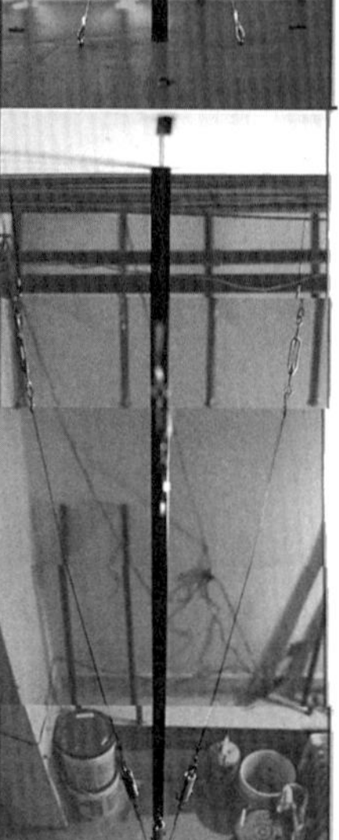
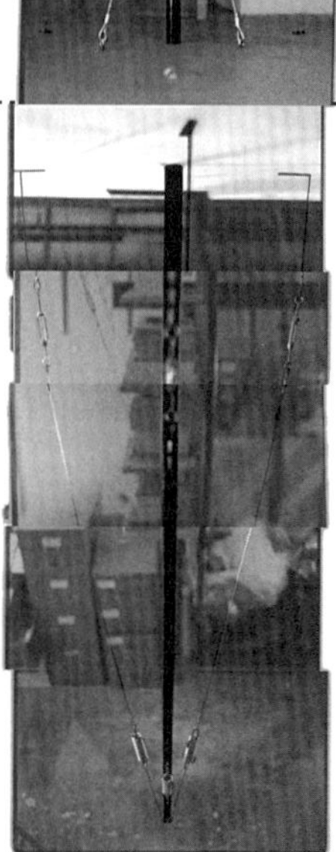
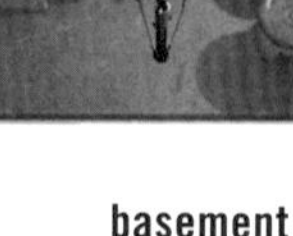
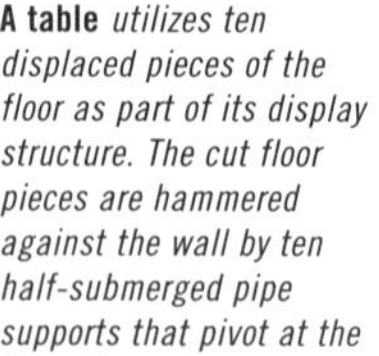

basement

A table *utilizes ten displaced pieces of the floor as part of its display structure. The cut floor pieces are hammered against the wall by ten half-submerged pipe supports that pivot at the floor joists.*

A bookshelf *adjacent to the reception desk slides vertically on a pipe between the gallery and basement. The shelf moves in relation to the weight of the books displayed above and stored below. As the books are sold the shelf rises back up into the gallery.*

Three stools *are fastened to metal pipes that penetrate through the floor into the basement. Springs and cables, which run from the base of the pipes back to the floor of the gallery, suspend the stools in dynamic equilibrium. Body weight produces vertical movement in the stools, bringing to play the presence of the basement. Reciprocally, the occupation of the stools is perceivable as movement in the basement below. The movement becomes a registration of the sitter's weight.*

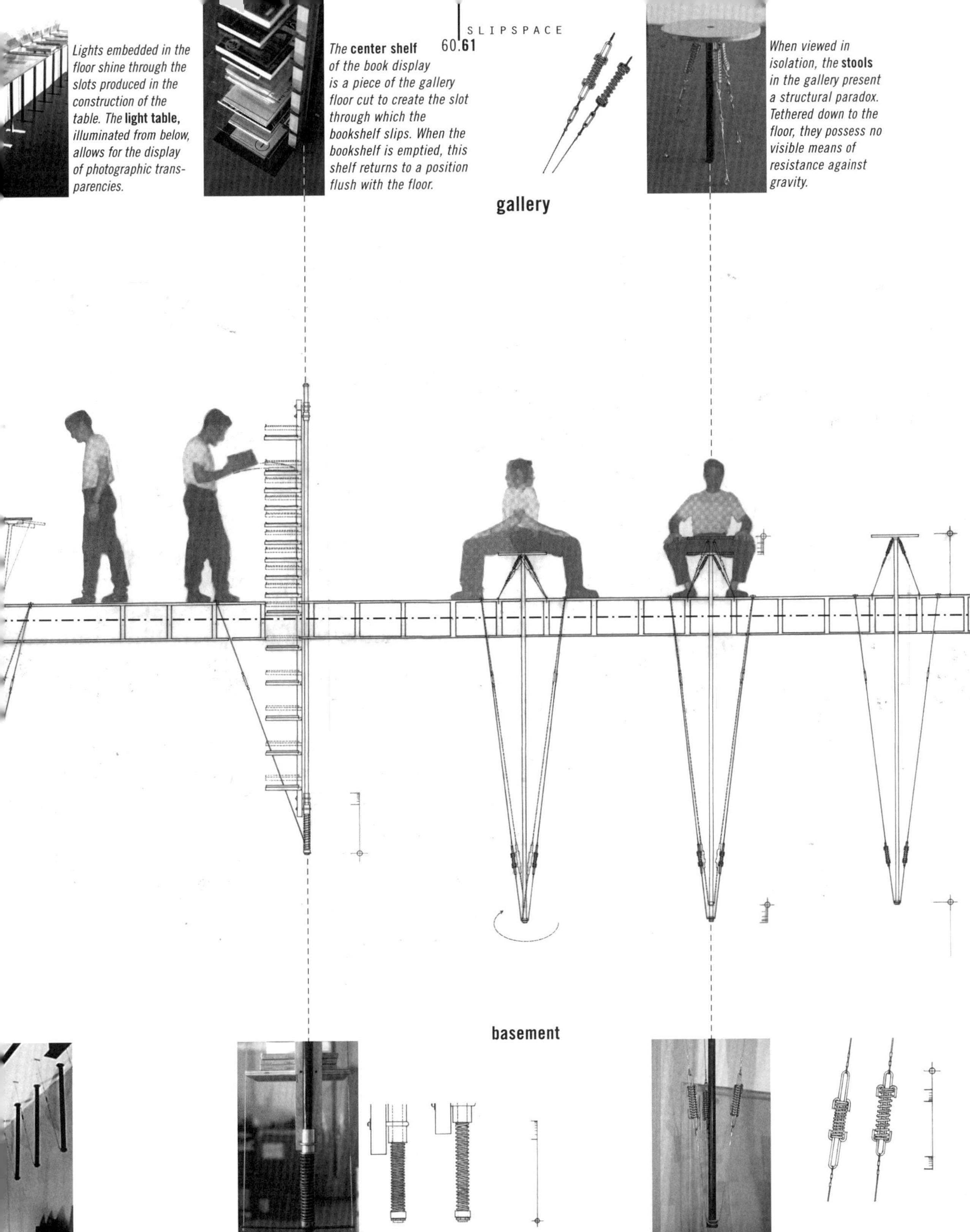

Lights embedded in the floor shine through the slots produced in the construction of the table. The **light table,** *illuminated from below, allows for the display of photographic transparencies.*

The **center shelf** *of the book display is a piece of the gallery floor cut to create the slot through which the bookshelf slips. When the bookshelf is emptied, this shelf returns to a position flush with the floor.*

When viewed in isolation, the **stools** *in the gallery present a structural paradox. Tethered down to the floor, they possess no visible means of resistance against gravity.*

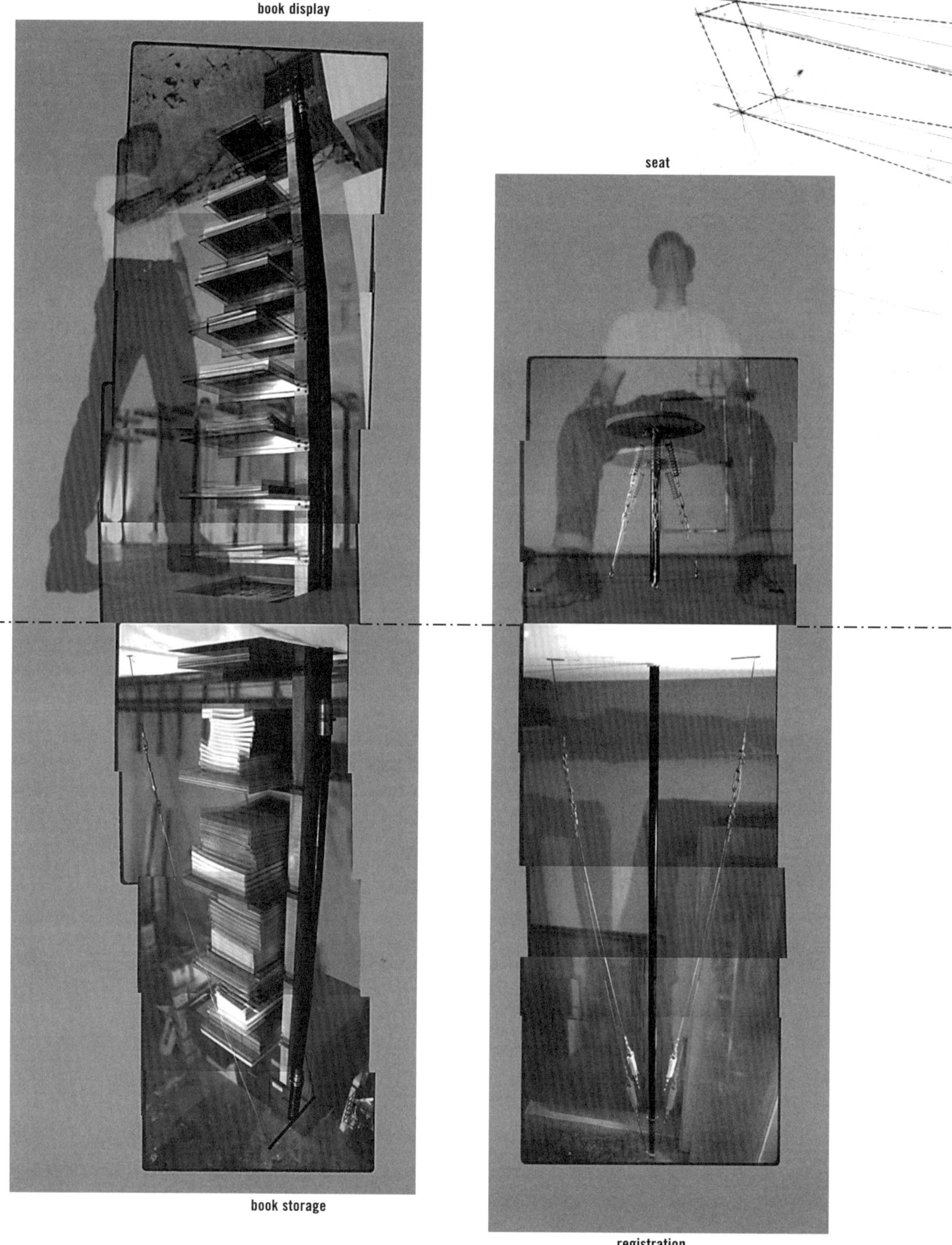
book display
seat
book storage
registration

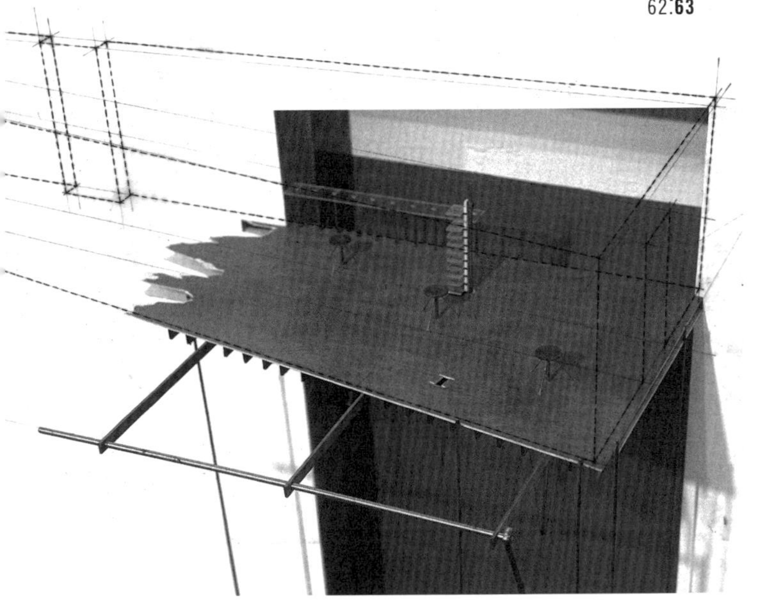

gallery

basement

A model *of the original installation, itself a part of the new installation, plays upon the disjunction between the object and its representation. A notational system of interconnecting wires and lines links the location of the full-scale project (still identifiable as scars in the plywood floor) and the objects in the model. Elevated to a suitable viewing height, the model is illuminated from a cut in the gallery floor that corresponds to its dimensions.*

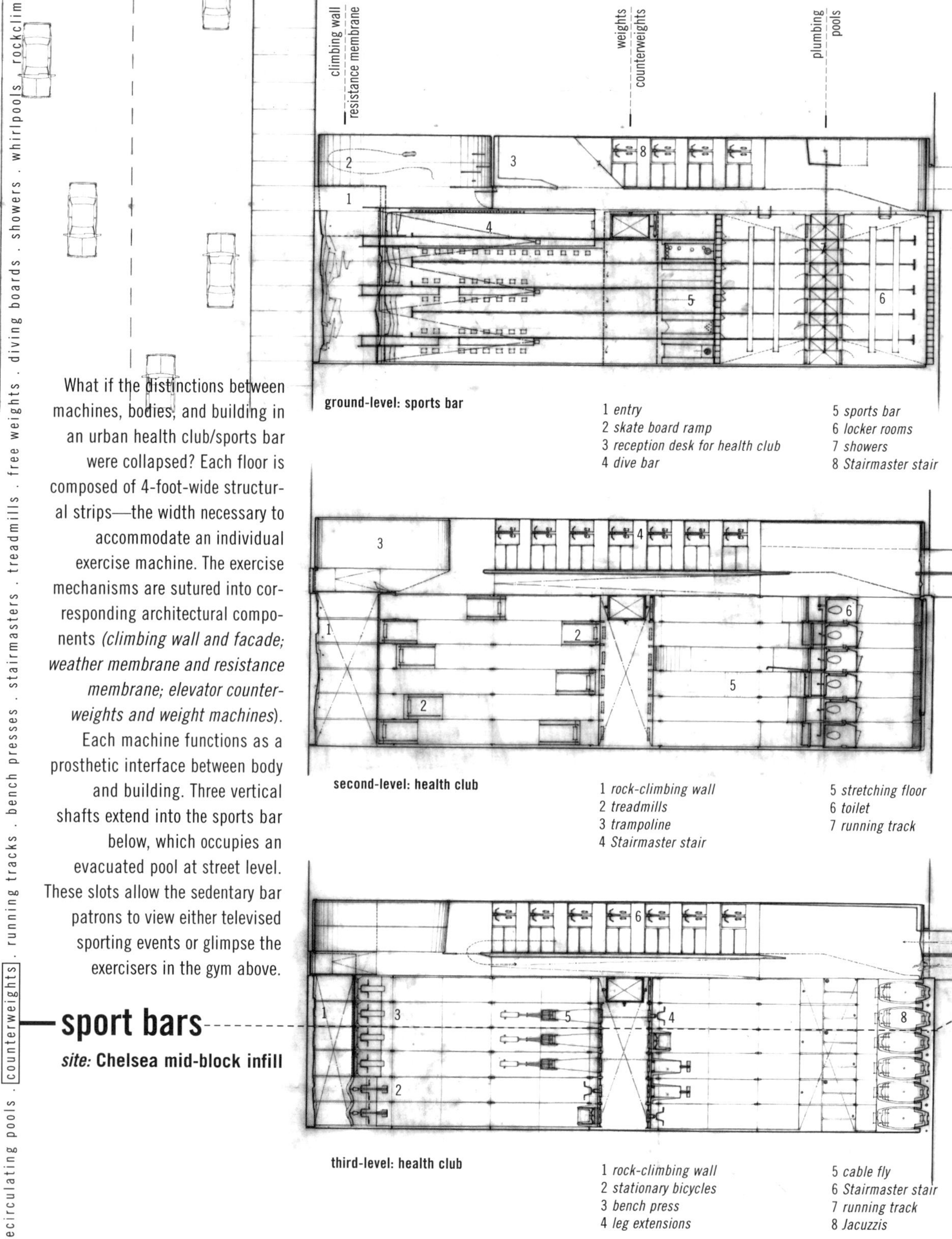

What if the distinctions between machines, bodies, and building in an urban health club/sports bar were collapsed? Each floor is composed of 4-foot-wide structural strips—the width necessary to accommodate an individual exercise machine. The exercise mechanisms are sutured into corresponding architectural components *(climbing wall and facade; weather membrane and resistance membrane; elevator counterweights and weight machines*). Each machine functions as a prosthetic interface between body and building. Three vertical shafts extend into the sports bar below, which occupies an evacuated pool at street level. These slots allow the sedentary bar patrons to view either televised sporting events or glimpse the exercisers in the gym above.

sport bars

***site:* Chelsea mid-block infill**

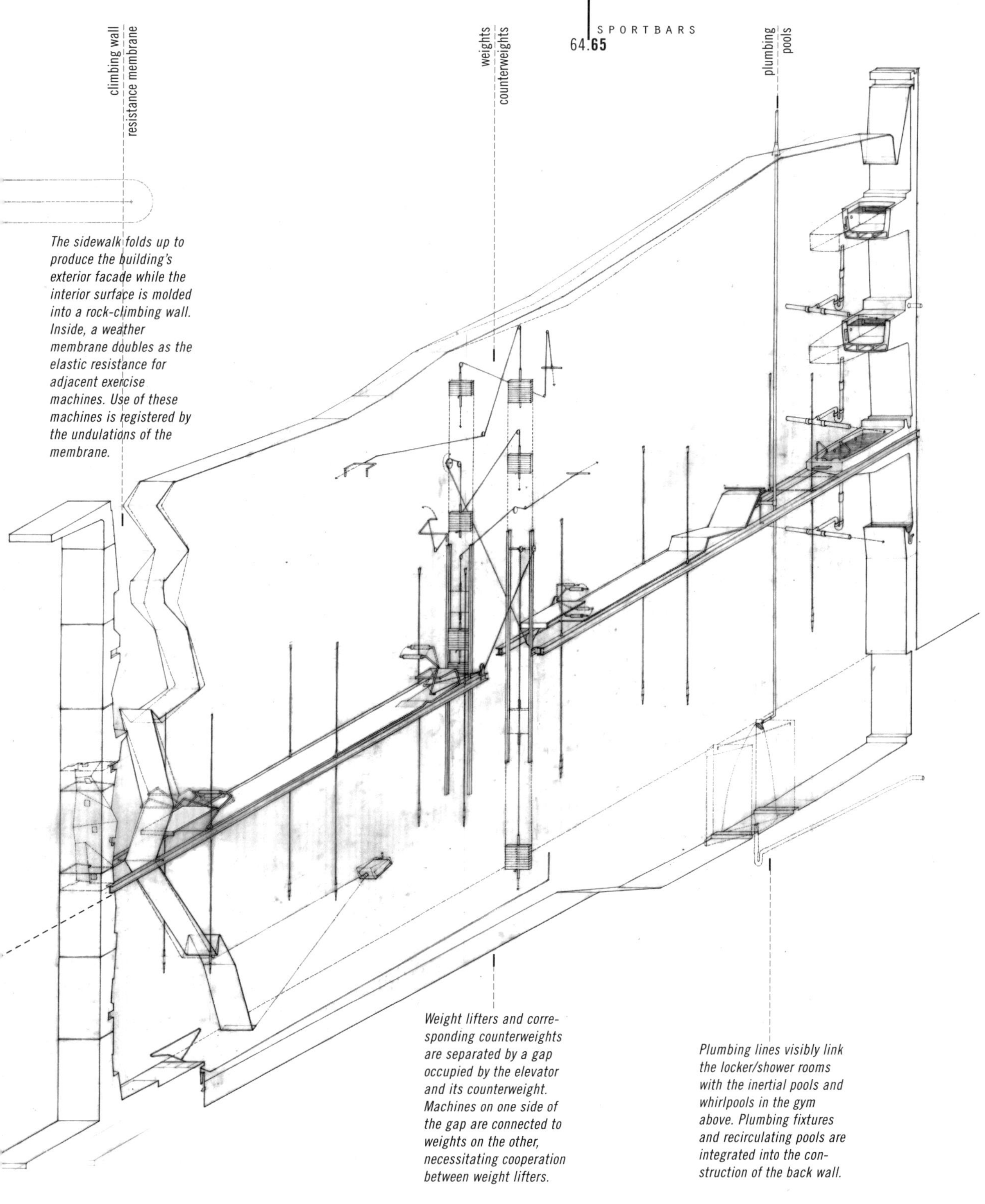

The sidewalk folds up to produce the building's exterior facade while the interior surface is molded into a rock-climbing wall. Inside, a weather membrane doubles as the elastic resistance for adjacent exercise machines. Use of these machines is registered by the undulations of the membrane.

Weight lifters and corresponding counterweights are separated by a gap occupied by the elevator and its counterweight. Machines on one side of the gap are connected to weights on the other, necessitating cooperation between weight lifters.

Plumbing lines visibly link the locker/shower rooms with the inertial pools and whirlpools in the gym above. Plumbing fixtures and recirculating pools are integrated into the construction of the back wall.

oblique projection of an exercise strip

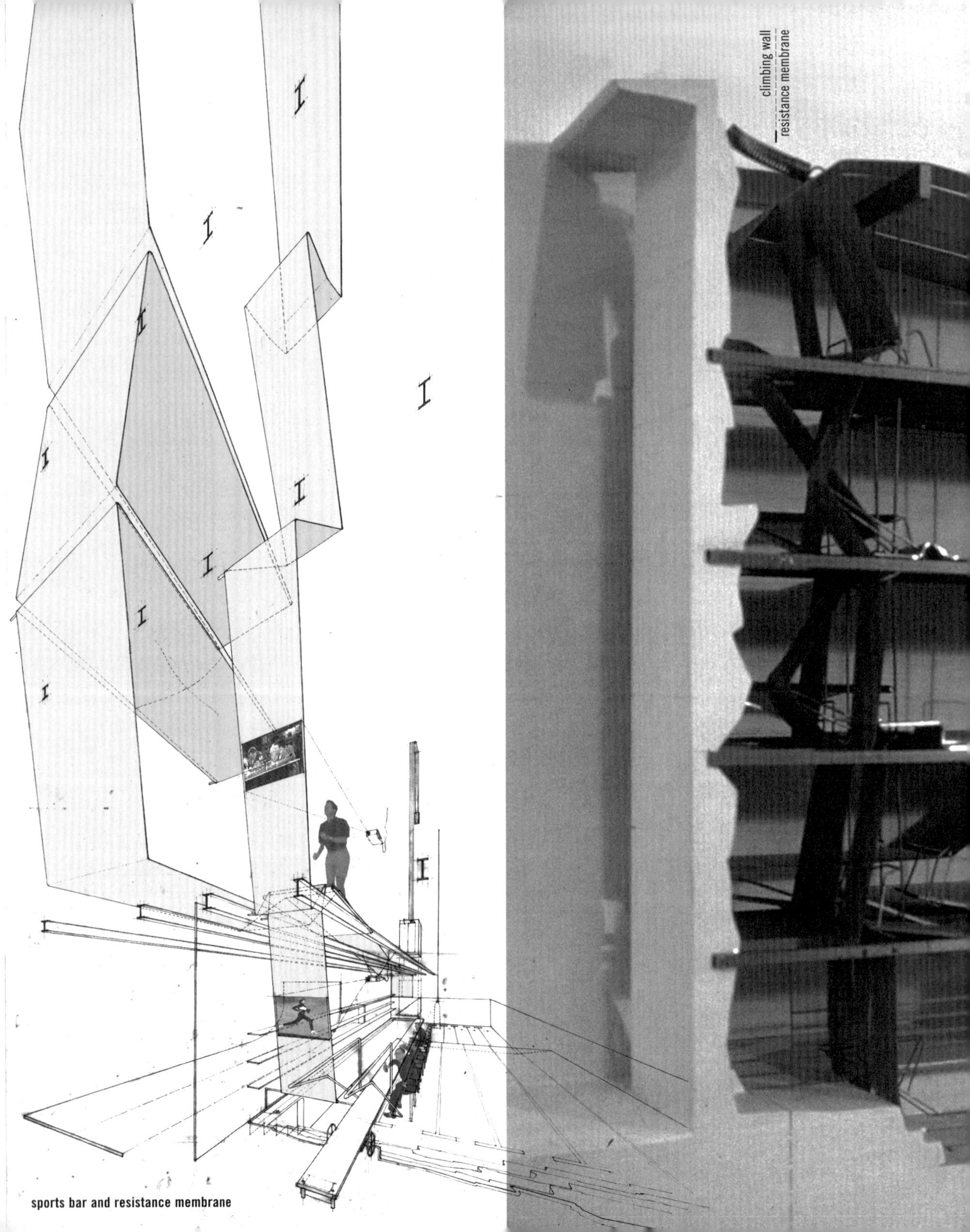

sports bar and resistance membrane

weights
counterweights

plumbing
pools

steel and rubber model

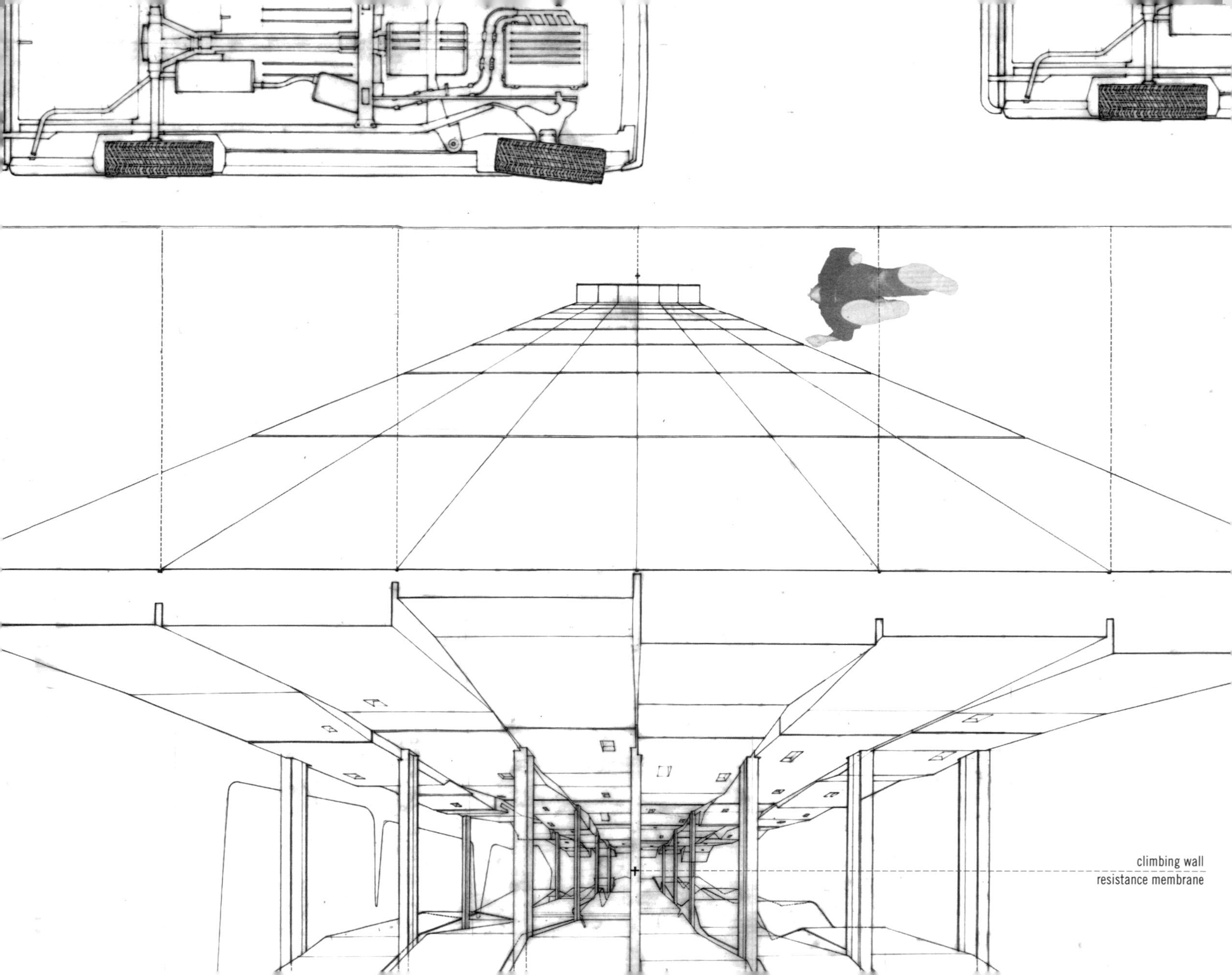
climbing wall
resistance membrane

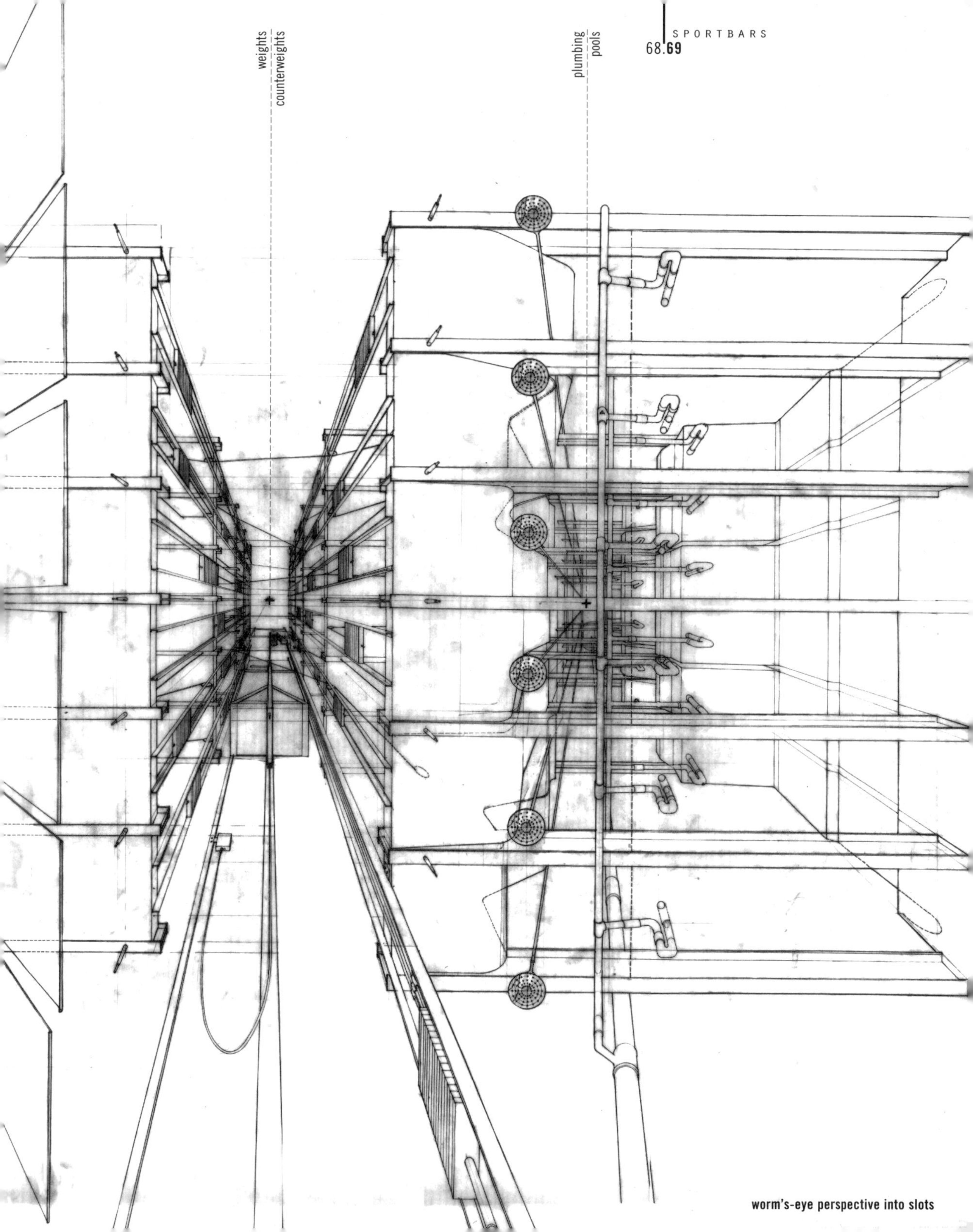

worm's-eye perspective into slots

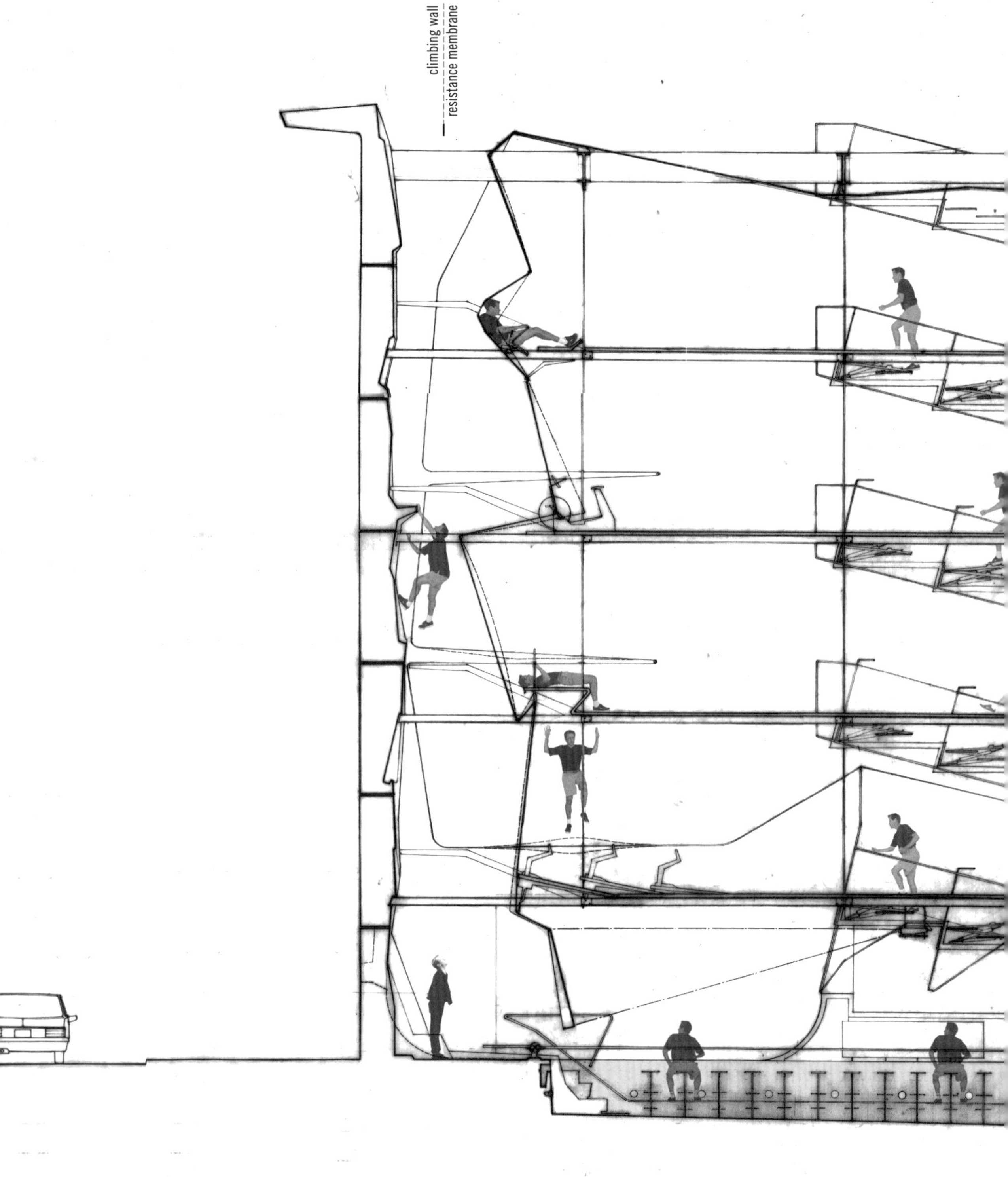

section

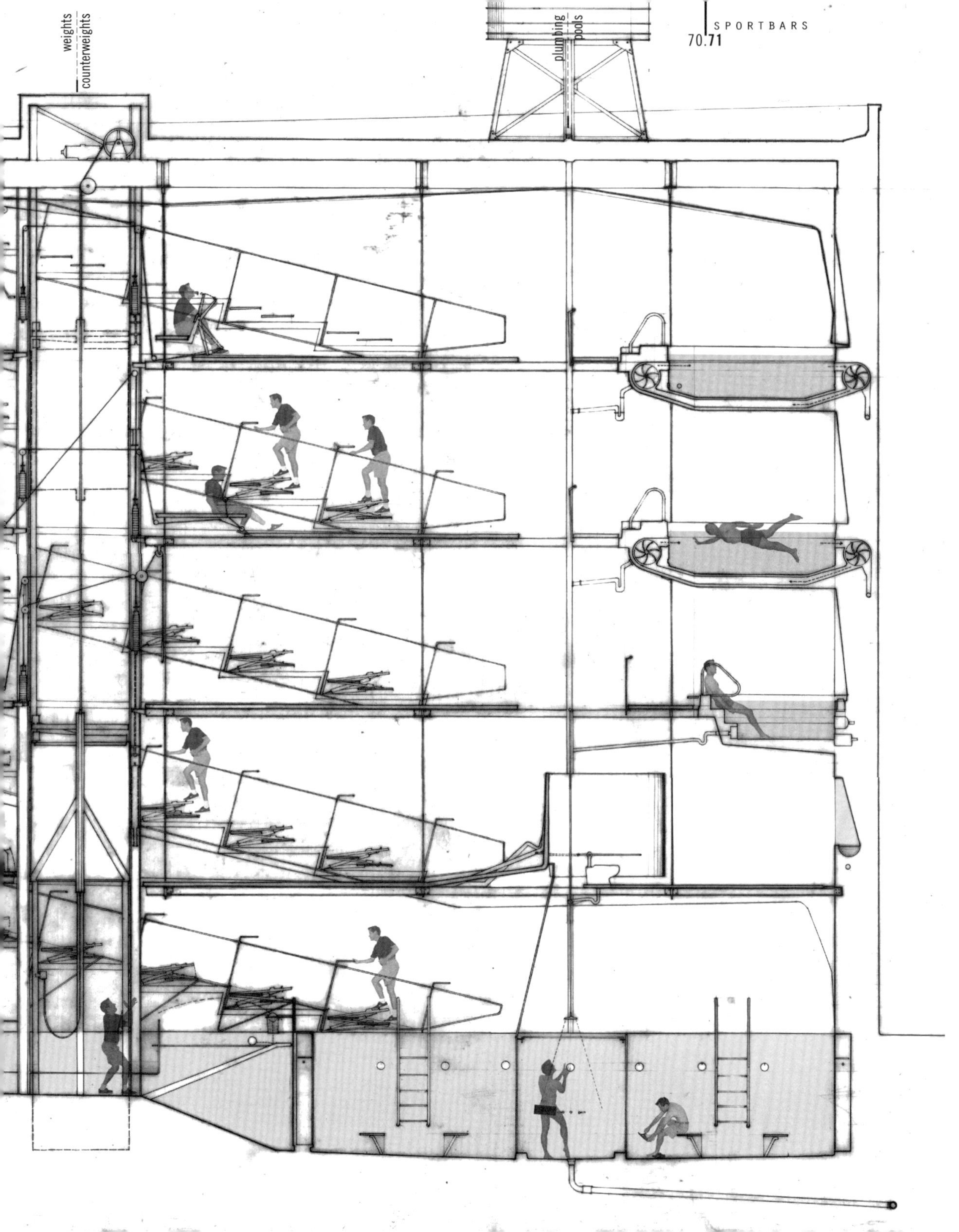
weights
counterweights
plumbing
pools

What if the spaces associated with the mutually dependent media of film and video are programatically crossbred? The public spectacle of movie-going and the individual ritual of video selection are spliced together along a continuous seam, allowing for visual, auditory, and spatial exchanges. Individual movie theaters are stacked with their screens forming an animated facade. The video store

video . filmplex

***site:* Cooper Square**

sneaks into the movies, occupying the space between the stacked theaters. When seen from the video store, the current movies are framed as previews for forthcoming video releases.

film		*video*
$250.2 *	***Men in Black***	$134.6 *
$229.1	***The Lost World***	$166.5
$181.4	***Liar Liar***	$103.3
$138.3	***Star Wars*** (re-release)	$60.9
$100.8	***Contact***	$35.8
$67.2	***Dante's Peak***	$34.7
$53.9	***Austin Powers***	$21.6
$8.1	***Turbo: Power Rangers***	$20.0

**gross receipts in millions. source:* Entertainment Weekly, *30 January 1997.*

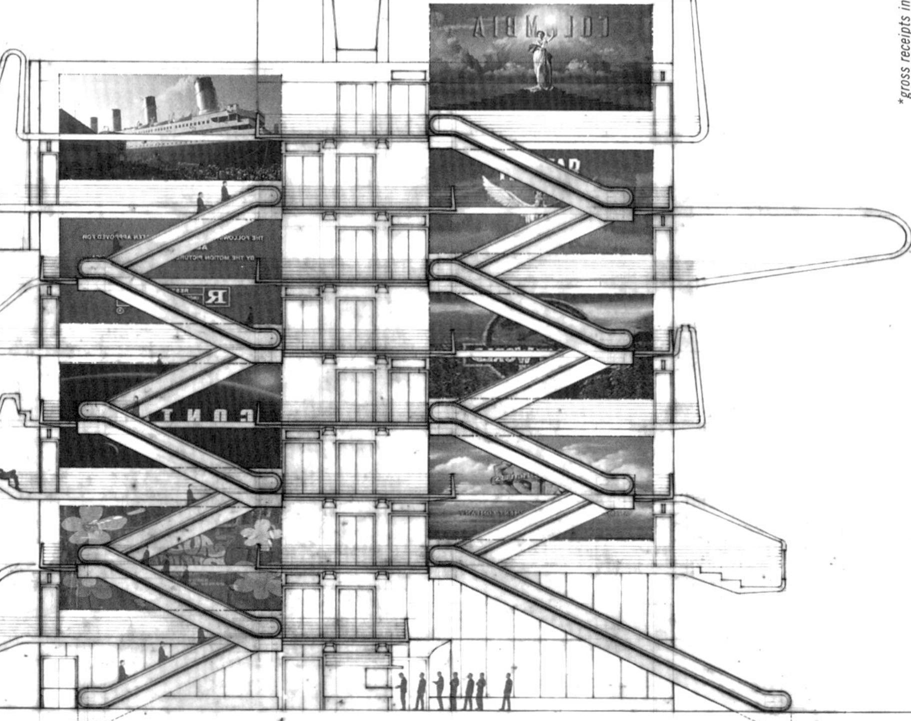

marquee facade

8:45 *pm*

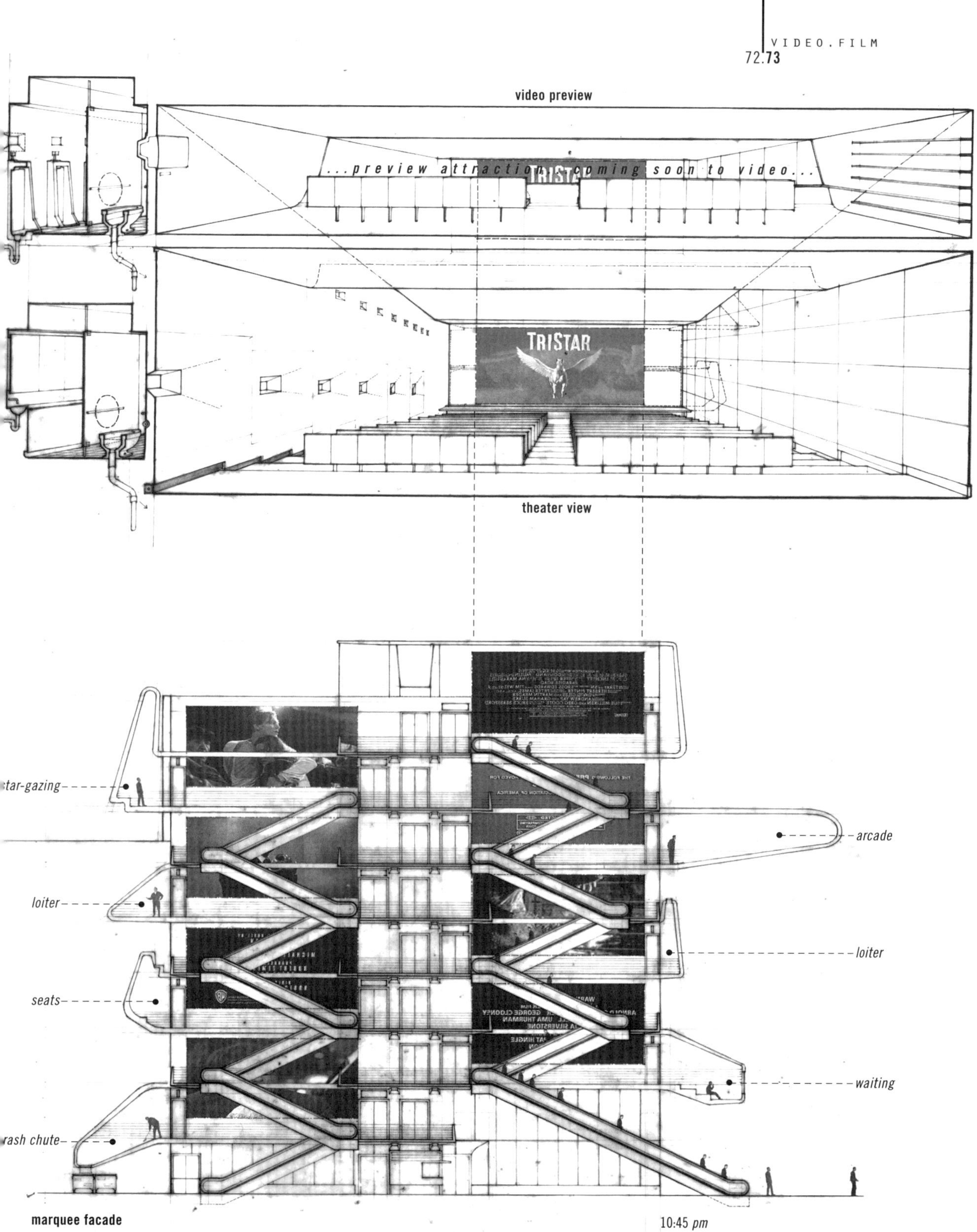
video preview
...preview attraction... coming soon to video...
TRISTAR
theater view
star-gazing
arcade
loiter
loiter
seats
waiting
trash chute
marquee facade
10:45 pm

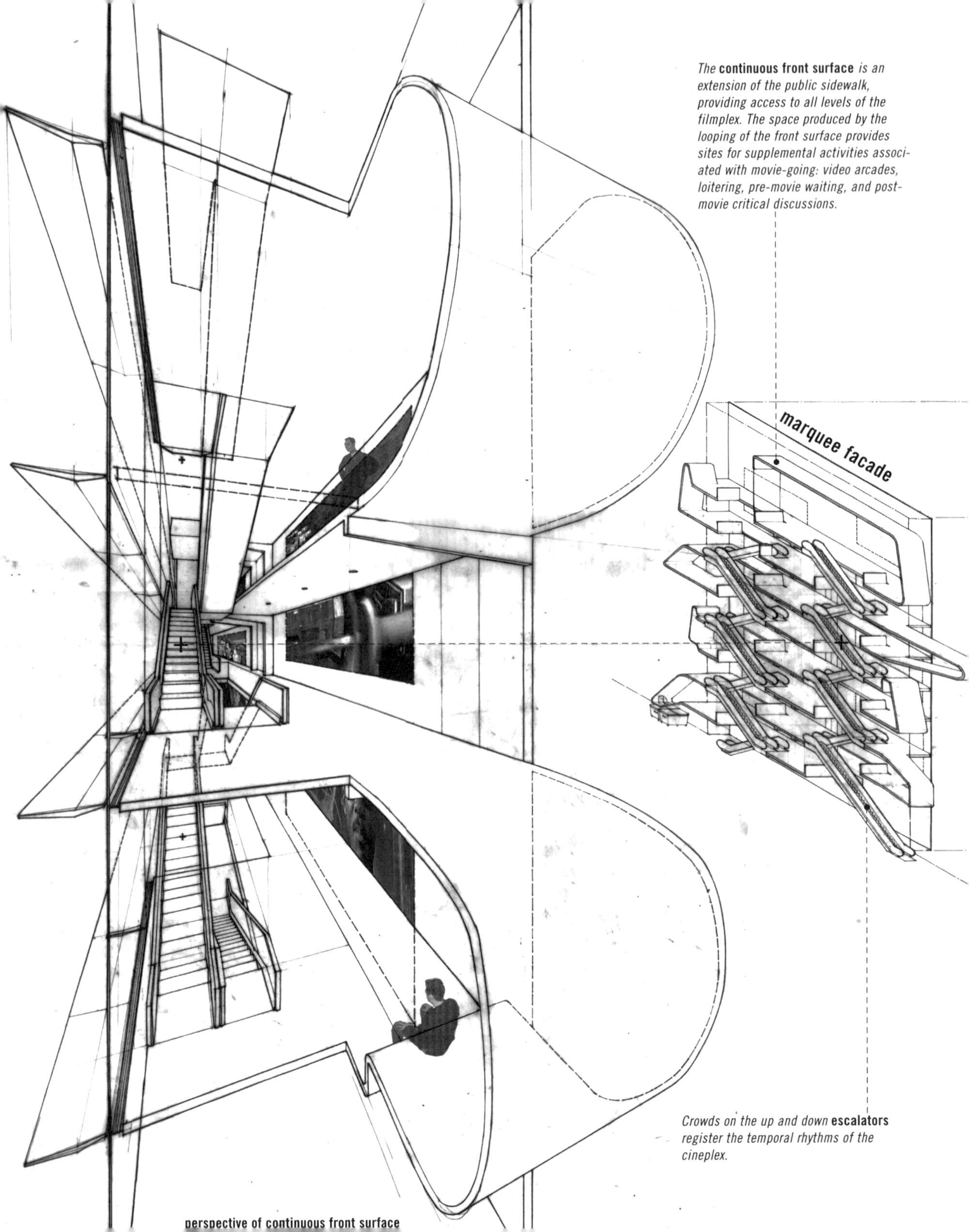

The **continuous front surface** *is an extension of the public sidewalk, providing access to all levels of the filmplex. The space produced by the looping of the front surface provides sites for supplemental activities associated with movie-going: video arcades, loitering, pre-movie waiting, and post-movie critical discussions.*

Crowds on the up and down **escalators** *register the temporal rhythms of the cineplex.*

perspective of continuous front surface

Sandwiched between the theaters are a series of **restrooms**. Each toilet stall has a one-way window, allowing a box-seat view into the movie. One never has to miss a moment of the film for the demands of the body. The designation of men's and women's rooms can be strategically arranged to accommodate Hollywood's gendering assumptions. Stalls in men's rooms look into action blockbusters, while women's rooms allow privileged views into costume dramas and romances. Ticket-line debates between couples are now mitigated.

An **outdoor cinema** at the level of the roof is equipped with retractable bleachers and a lawn for use during summer months.

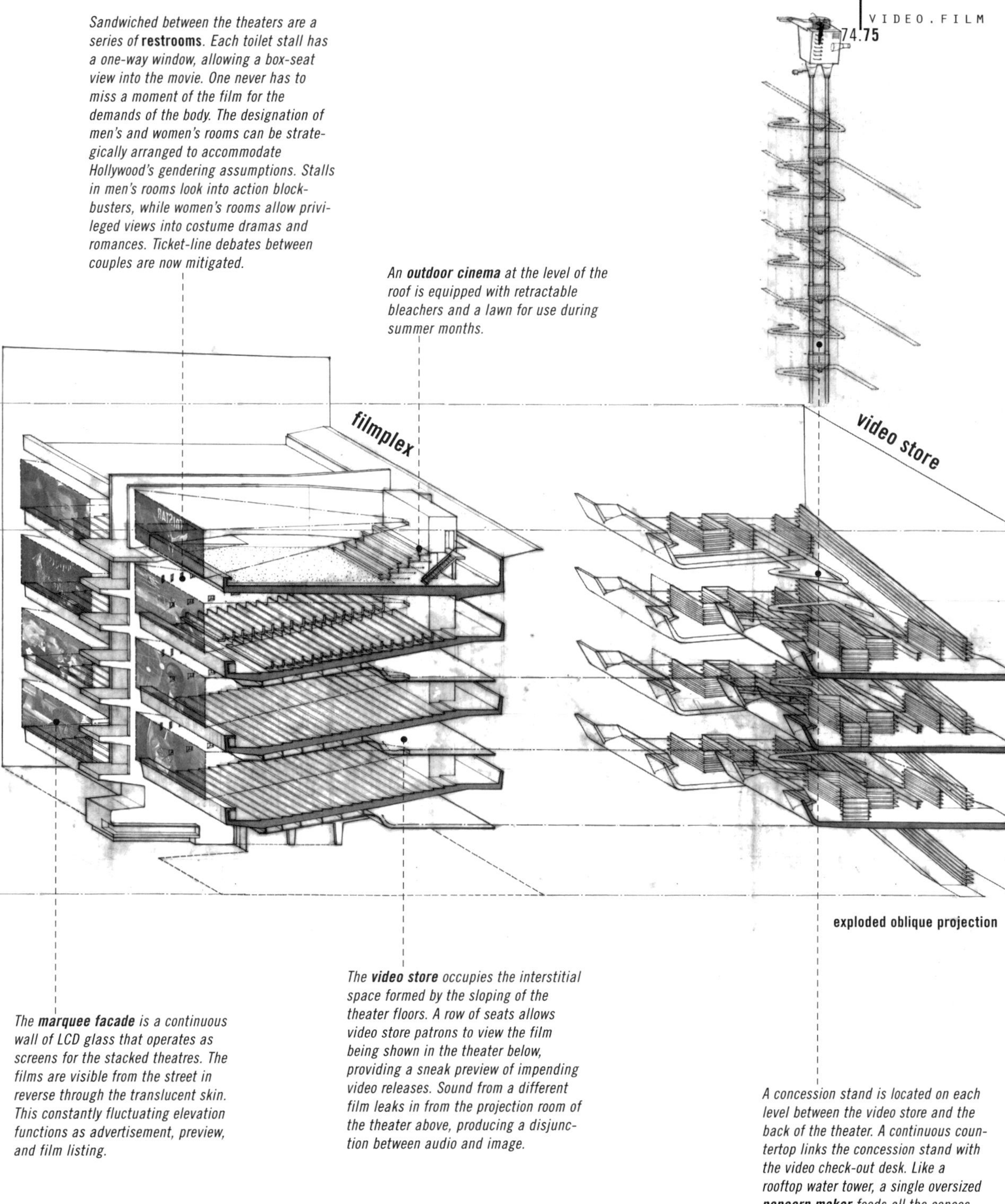

exploded oblique projection

The **marquee facade** is a continuous wall of LCD glass that operates as screens for the stacked theatres. The films are visible from the street in reverse through the translucent skin. This constantly fluctuating elevation functions as advertisement, preview, and film listing.

The **video store** occupies the interstitial space formed by the sloping of the theater floors. A row of seats allows video store patrons to view the film being shown in the theater below, providing a sneak preview of impending video releases. Sound from a different film leaks in from the projection room of the theater above, producing a disjunction between audio and image.

A concession stand is located on each level between the video store and the back of the theater. A continuous countertop links the concession stand with the video check-out desk. Like a rooftop water tower, a single oversized **popcorn maker** feeds all the concession stands with fresh popcorn and hot butter, and permeates the whole interior with its luscious odor.

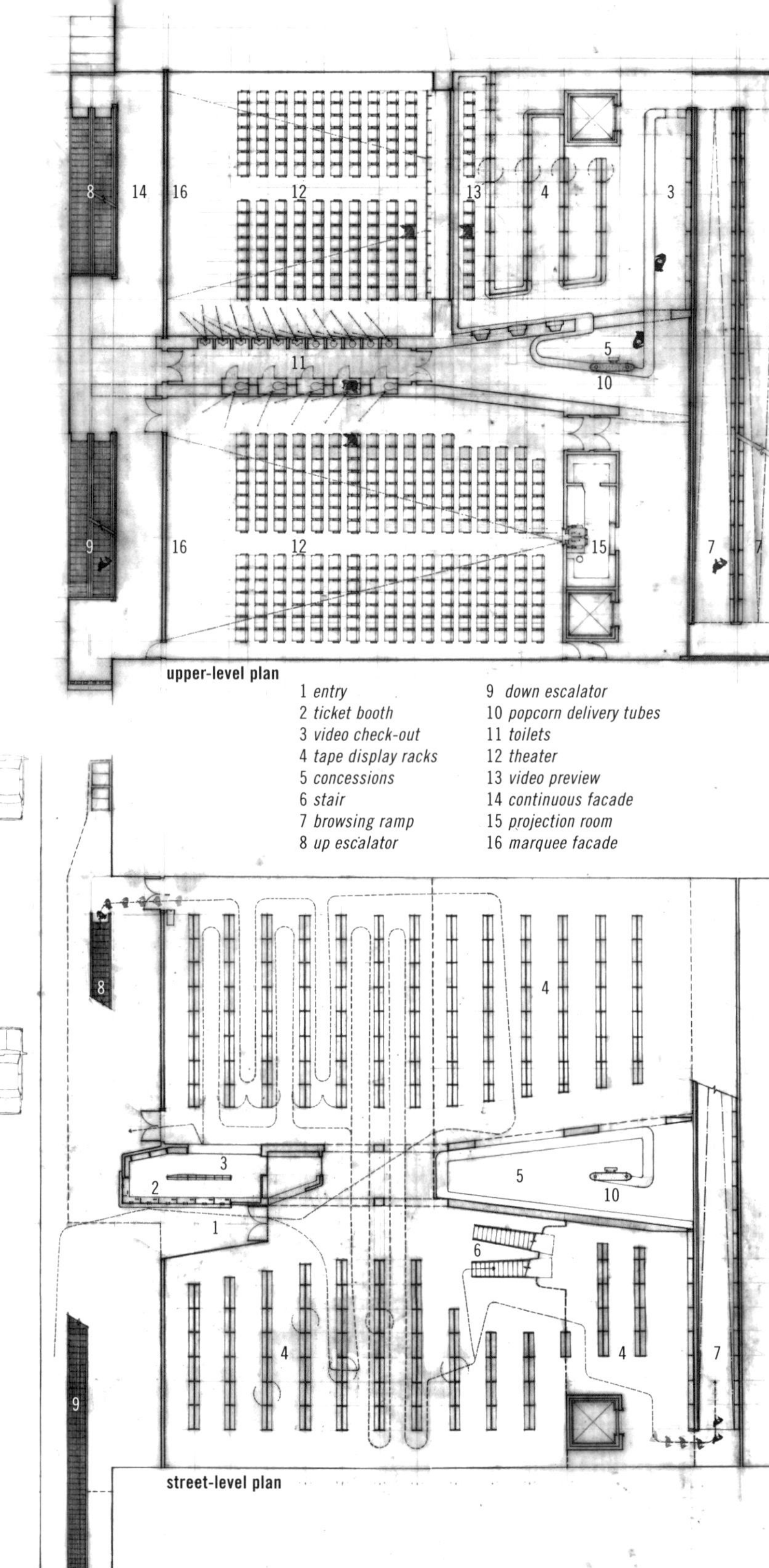

upper-level plan

1 *entry*
2 *ticket booth*
3 *video check-out*
4 *tape display racks*
5 *concessions*
6 *stair*
7 *browsing ramp*
8 *up escalator*
9 *down escalator*
10 *popcorn delivery tubes*
11 *toilets*
12 *theater*
13 *video preview*
14 *continuous facade*
15 *projection room*
16 *marquee facade*

street-level plan

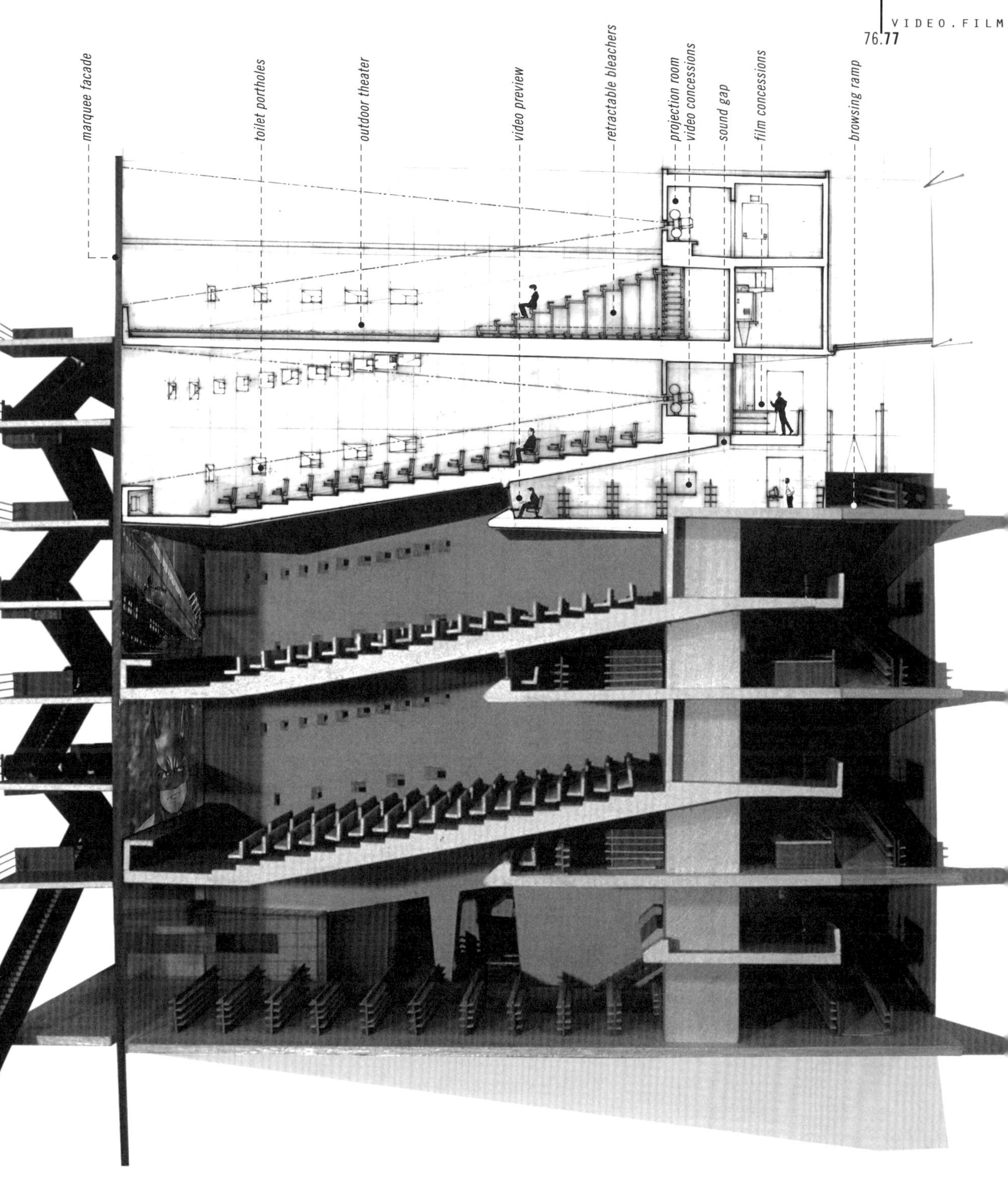

section model

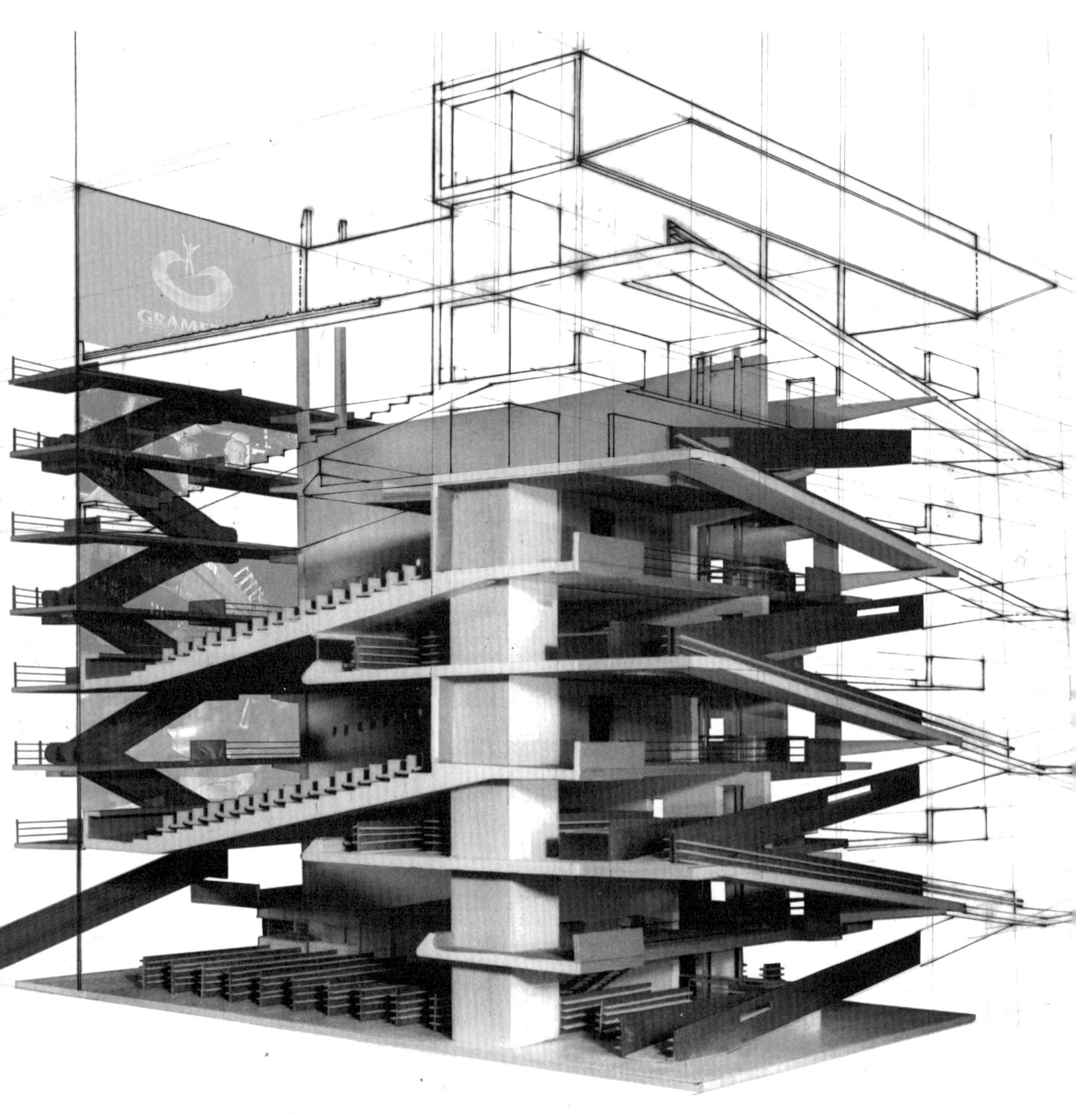

composite model / perspective

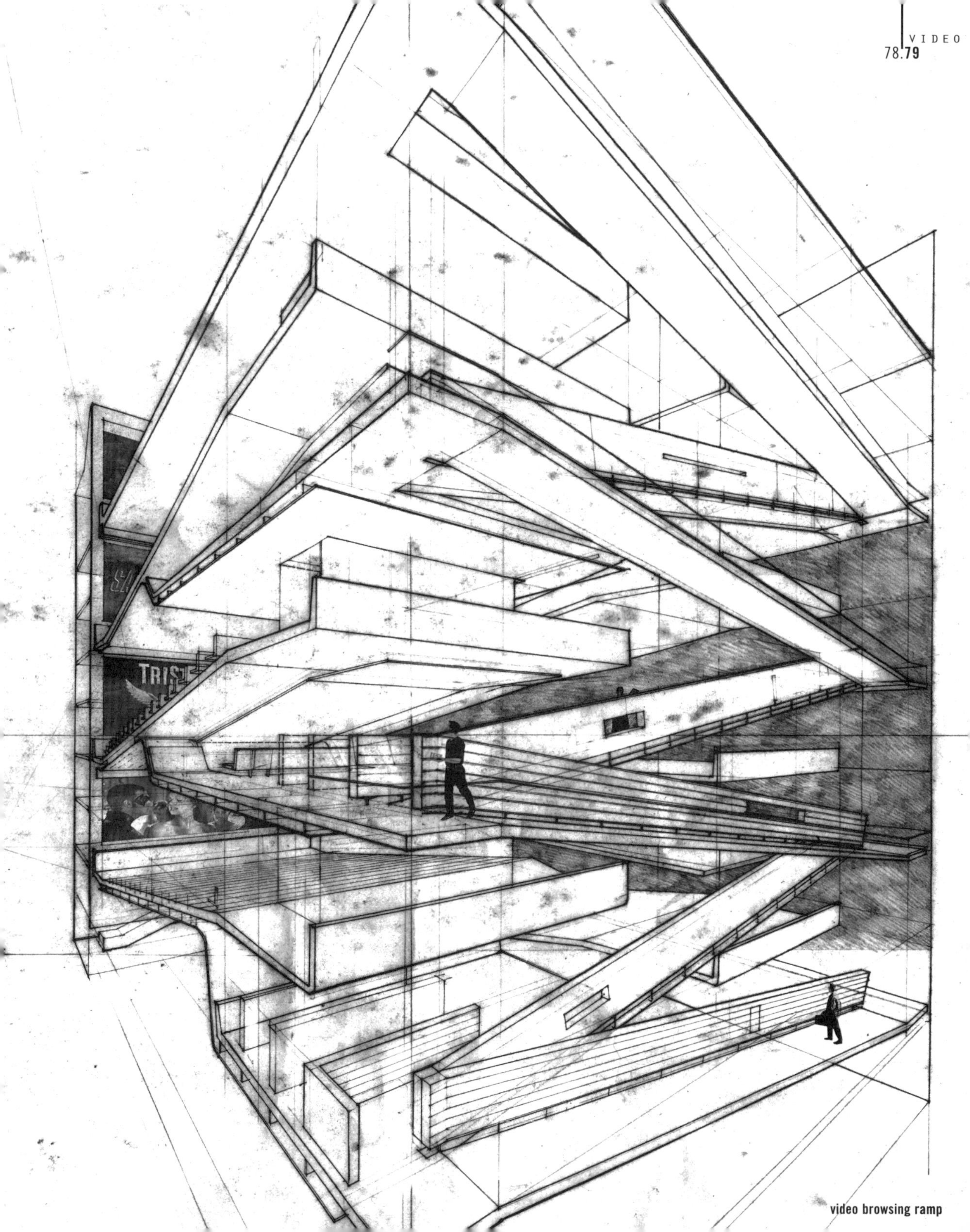

video browsing ramp

acknowledgments

pull of beauty

StoreFront for Art and Architecture
February 13–March 30, 1996
gallery co-directors:
Shirin Neshat
Kyong Park
collaborator:
Peter Pelsinski
curators:
Victoria Milne
Kiki Smith
metal fabrication:
Richard Goloveyko
wood fabrication:
Robert Kulka
installation assistance:
Stephanie Baffler
Carmen Lenzi
Joanne Liou
Michael Meredith
Hilary Sample
Karen Stonely
Nicholas Tobier
Kim Yao

testing 1..2..3..

StoreFront for Art and Architecture
June 12–August 2, 1997
gallery co-directors:
Shirin Neshat
Kyong Park
installation collaborator:
Deane Simpson
installation assistance:
Patrice Gardera
Rachael Gray
Janette Kim
Carmen Lenzi
Lynn Sullivan
Alexandra Ultsch
Kim Yao

eavesdropping

Exit Art/The First World
September 21–October 19, 1996
gallery co-directors/curators:
Jeanette Ingberman
Papo Colo
installation assistance:
Chris Korsch
Bill Peterson
Clarissa Richardson
David Ruff
Mark Shephard
Jennifer Whitburn
Kim Yao

skyfill . landfill

Van Alen Institute Competition
for Governors Island, 1996

slip space

StoreFront for Art and Architecture
March 12–April 16, 1994
gallery co-directors:
Shirin Neshat
Kyong Park
collaborator:
Peter Pelsinski
curators:
Beatriz Colomina
Dennis Dollens
Cindi Patton
Eve Kosofsky Sedgwick
Henry Urbach
Mark Wigley

Pamphlet Architecture was initiated in 1977 as an independent vehicle to criticize, question, and exchange views. Each issue is assembled by an individual author/architect. For more information, pamphlet proposals, or contributions, please write to:

Pamphlet Architecture
c/o Princeton Architectural Press
37 East Seventh Street
New York, NY 10003

Previously Published:

1.	*Bridges*	S. Holl	1977*
2.	*10 Californian Houses*	M. Mack	1978*
3.	*Villa Prima Facie*	L. Lerup	1978*
4.	*Stairwells*	L. Dimitriu	1979*
5.	*The Alphabetical City*	S. Holl	1980
6.	*Einstein Tomb*	L. Woods	1980*
7.	*Bridge of Houses*	S. Holl	1981*
8.	*Planetary Architecture*	Z. Hadid	1981*
9.	*Rural and Urban House Types*	S. Holl	1983
10.	*Metafisica Della Architettura*	A. Sartoris	1984*
11.	*Hybrid Buildings*	J. Fenton	1985
12.	*Building;Machines*	R. McCarter	1987
13.	*Edge of a City*	S. Holl	1991
14.	*Mosquitoes*	K. Kaplan/T. Krueger	1993
15.	*War and Architecture*	L. Woods	1993
16.	*Architecture as a Translation of Music*	E. Martin	1994
17.	*Small Buildings*	M. Cadwell	1996
19.	*Reading Drawing Building*	M. Silver	1996
20.	*Seven Partly Underground Rooms*	M. Ray	1997

The first ten pamphlets—eight of which are out-of-print—are available in their entirety in the collection *Pamphlet Architecture 1 Through 10.*

*out of print